Jimm Stallings
2/8/16

# Systematic Theology

## VOLUME VIII

### BIOGRAPHICAL SKETCH AND INDEXES

By

## LEWIS SPERRY CHAFER, D.D., Litt.D., Th.D.

*President and Professor of Systematic Theology*
*Dallas Theological Seminary*

*PUBLISHED BY*

## DALLAS SEMINARY PRESS

### DALLAS, TEXAS

PRINTED IN THE UNITED STATES OF AMERICA
BY THE VAIL-BALLOU PRESS, INC., BINGHAMTON, N. Y.

# ACKNOWLEDGMENT

Grateful appreciation is extended for permission to use quotations from books copyrighted by the publishers and authors listed below:

D. Appleton-Century Company, Inc.—*The New Century Dictionary.*

John W. Bradbury—contribution written especially for this work.

Encyclopaedia Britannica, Inc.—*Encyclopaedia Britannica.*

Dr. E. Schuyler English—*Studies in the Gospel according to Matthew.*

Wm. B. Eerdmans Publishing Co.—*International Standard Bible Encyclopaedia.*

Funk & Wagnalls Co.—*New Standard Dictionary.*

Dr. Norman B. Harrison, The Harrison Service—*His Love.*

Loizeaux Brothers, Inc.—*Notes on Genesis,* by C. H. Mackintosh; *Notes on Exodus,* by C. H. Mackintosh; *Notes on Leviticus,* by C. H. Mackintosh; *Synopsis of the Books of the Bible,* by J. N. Darby; *Lectures on Daniel,* by H. A. Ironside; *Lectures on Revelation,* by H. A. Ironside; *Notes on Proverbs,* by H. A. Ironside; *Notes on the Minor Prophets,* by H. A. Ironside.

Moody Press—*Isaac and Rebekah,* by George E. Guille; *Scofield Correspondence Course.*

Dr. William R. Newell—*Romans Verse by Verse.*

Erling C. Olsen—*Meditations in the Psalms, Walks with Our Lord through John's Gospel.*

Our Hope—*Angels of God,* by A. C. Gaebelein; *Studies in Zechariah,* by A. C. Gaebelein; *Satan, His Person, His Work and His Destiny,* by F. C. Jennings; *Imperialism and Christ,* by Ford C. Ottman; *Unfolding the Ages,* by Ford C. Ottman.

Oxford University Press—*Biblical Doctrines,* by B. B. Warfield; *Christology and Criticism,* by B. B. Warfield; *Revelation and Inspiration,* by B. B. Warfield; *Studies in Theology,* by B. B. Warfield.

Fleming H. Revell Co.—*Christian Worker's Commentary,* by James M. Gray.

Charles Scribner's Sons—*The Sermon on the Mount,* by Martin Dibelius.

The Sunday School Times Co.—*The Sunday School Times*.

Dr. John F. Walvoord—*Outline of Christology; The Doctrine of the Holy Spirit*.

Zondervan Publishing House—*The Critical and Explanatory Commentary*, by Jamieson, Fausset & Brown.

---

In the preparation of the indexes, the author was assisted by Mr. John A. Witmer, A.M., Th. M.

# TABLE OF CONTENTS

Biographical Sketch                                    3

Table of Contents, Volume I                            9

Table of Contents, Volume II                          22

Table of Contents, Volume III                         28

Table of Contents, Volume IV                          38

Table of Contents, Volume V                           51

Table of Contents, Volume VI                          56

Table of Contents, Volume VII                         61

Author Index                                          67

Scripture Index                                       99

Subject Index                                        115

# BIOGRAPHICAL SKETCH

# BIOGRAPHICAL SKETCH OF THE AUTHOR

By

## C. F. LINCOLN, A.M., Th.D.

*Treasurer and Professor of English Bible*
*Dallas Theological Seminary*

The Reverend Lewis Sperry Chafer, D.D., Litt.D., was born at Rock Creek, Ashtabula County, Ohio, on February 27, 1871. He was reared in a devout Christian home, his immediate ancestors having been faithful ministers of the gospel.

His father, the Reverend Thomas Franklin Chafer, was graduated during the presidency of Jacob Tuckerman from Farmer's College, College Hill, Cincinnati, and from Auburn Theological Seminary with the class of 1864. He was born in the year 1829 and died during the fifty-third year of his life, in 1882, when Dr. Chafer was eleven years of age. William Chafer, the father of Thomas Franklin Chafer, and the paternal grandfather of Dr. Chafer, was born in York, England, and moved to the United States in the year 1837, when his son Thomas was eight years of age. He took up residence in the state of Kentucky and was long dedicated to farming in that section of the country.

Dr. Chafer's mother was Lois Lomira Sperry. She was born at Rock Creek, Ohio, on June 3, 1836, and died in the fall of the year 1915 at the age of seventy-nine when Dr. Chafer was forty-four years of age. Her father, Asa Sperry, was a licensed Welsh Wesleyan preacher, though he was a harness-maker by trade. Ann Sperry, of Irish descent, was the maternal grandmother of Dr. Chafer.

As a boy, Dr. Chafer attended the public schools of Rock Creek until he attained the age of twelve years. After that, from 1885 to 1888, he attended New Lyme Institute of New Lyme, Ohio. There was an orchestra or choral society at that institution and as a young student he was there first introduced to the serious study of music, in which art he became remarkably proficient. Later, when his widowed mother had removed to Oberlin, Ohio, for the education of her three children, as a young man Dr. Chafer attended Oberlin College and Conserv-

3

atory of Music from 1889 to 1892. It was at Oberlin that Dr. Chafer met Ella Loraine Case, a devoted student of music and a deeply spiritual-minded young lady who later became his beloved wife and faithful lifelong companion and coworker. At this time Dr. Chafer began travelling as a gospel singer with Evangelist Arthur T. Reed. This ministry continued for a period of about seven years, though during that time he was engaged to direct gospel music for other evangelists also. On April 22, 1896, Dr. Chafer was united in marriage to Miss Case whose home was in Ellington, Chautauqua County, New York. She at once took an active part in the ministry to which her husband was devoted, laboring with him as soloist and accompanist at the piano; in both of these services she was exceptionally gifted and thoroughly trained. In 1897, the year following his marriage, Dr. Chafer began his service as an evangelist, ministering in this work until the year 1914 both by preaching and singing. In the year 1900 Dr. Chafer was ordained to the gospel ministry by a Council of Congregational Ministers in the First Congregational Church of Buffalo. In 1903, due to his having taken up residence in East Northfield, Massachusetts, his ministerial relationship was removed to the Presbytery of Troy, New York. At that time Dr. C. I. Scofield was pastor of the Congregational Church of Northfield, which had been organized by D. L. Moody, and there was cemented between the two men a closeness of fellowship in the gospel that grew into an intimate companionship in the teaching ministry which lasted until Dr. Scofield's death in 1921. When Dr. Chafer moved to East Northfield he began at once his service as music leader, along with Ira Sankey, D. B. Towner, George Stebbins, and others, in the great Moody Summer Bible Conferences. Mrs. Chafer was official organist for the conferences. In the winter Dr. Chafer travelled out of Northfield in an ever widening evangelistic ministry, and his service in the Summer Conferences brought him into close touch with most of the great conservative Bible teachers of that period. In the year 1906 Dr. Chafer moved his ministerial relationship from the Troy Presbytery to that of the Orange Presbytery of North Carolina, and in the year 1916 he himself took up residence in East Orange, New Jersey. Some time after this, after a remarkable spiritual experience in the study of Dr. Scofield in Dallas, Texas, he definitely dedicated his life to an exacting study of the Bible. After an exceedingly fruitful Bible-teaching ministry which took him on repeated occasions to nearly every state in the union, Dr. Chafer removed to Dallas, Texas, in the year 1922, for the principal purpose of establishing the Dallas Theo-

logical Seminary. In the year 1924 the school was founded with the cooperation and advice of Dr. A. B. Winchester of Toronto, and Dr. W. H. Griffith Thomas of Philadelphia. Dr. Chafer was President of the Seminary from its beginning until the time of his death.

Dr. Chafer travelled in the ministry of Bible teaching in England, Scotland, Ireland, Belgium, and elsewhere. He always had a great missionary vision and served on various mission boards and visited mission fields in Europe, Mexico, and all of Central America where his counsel and ministry of Bible teaching and evangelistic service were of wonderful benefit to the missionaries and to the national churches.

Dr. Chafer was the author of many pamphlets and magazine articles and of the following books on Bible themes and doctrines: *Satan,* 1909; *True Evangelism,* 1911; *The Kingdom in History and Prophecy,* 1915; *Salvation,* 1916; *He That Is Spiritual,* 1918; *Grace,* 1922; *Major Bible Themes,* 1926; and *The Ephesian Letter,* 1935. These books have been before the Christian public in all English-speaking lands for many years and are still in constant and almost undiminished demand. Multiplied thousands have been blessed in spirit, instructed in the grace of God, and confirmed in the faith and in the assurance of salvation by the clear and forceful teaching set down by his able pen. A number of his books have been, or are being, translated on mission fields into several languages; thus a fruitful world-wide ministry has resulted.

From 1940 to 1952 Dr. Chafer was editor of *Bibliotheca Sacra,* the oldest theological quarterly in America.

The discipline and training which Dr. Chafer received as a background for the writing of this extensive work on Systematic Theology was that of many years of faithful study. In his early years he was known among Bible teachers as especially given to doctrine and was invited on several occasions to become teacher of Bible doctrine in leading institutes of this country.

When he undertook the professorship of Systematic Theology in the Seminary in Dallas, Texas, he at once gave himself to ceaseless study and reading in that division of ministerial training. He secured and became familiar with an exceedingly large library on Systematic Theology. The exercise of teaching this vast field of truth for many years required him to answer practically every question which students of serious mind could ask.

Dr. Chafer himself said that "the very fact that I did not study a prescribed course in theology made it possible for me to approach the

subject with an unprejudiced mind and to be concerned only with what the Bible actually teaches." This independent research has resulted in this work which is unabridged, Calvinistic, premillennial, and dispensational.

In fulfillment of Ephesians 4:8, 11, God gave a beloved "teacher" unto the Church. We are sure that through this treatise on Theology God's purpose in such a gift, as expressed in verses 12–16, will be further fulfilled to the people of God for immense blessing in "the body of Christ."

---

Dr. Chafer suffered a heart attack in California in the year 1935. Although that stroke was severe, by observing a careful regimen in his convalescence he recovered and gained strength for an active ministry until 1945 when again he was stricken in California. From this attack he did not have a full recovery, but after a period of time he was able to continue his classroom and platform ministry. A third attack in 1948 further weakened him, but he still continued his public work in a limited way until almost the close of his life.

In May, 1952, after his classes were finished at the Seminary he covered the cities in Pennsylvania known as the Harrisburg Circuit of Bible conferences and spoke at commencement and baccalaureate services at Grace Theological Seminary and Columbia Bible College. It seemed to us who were close to him that this pressing schedule with its nighttime train transfers and closely dated speaking engagements overtaxed his scant strength and carried him beyond the point of possible return to his normal ministry.

However, Dr. Chafer had often manifested that he desired to remain active in the Lord's work until the end. In June, 1952, following his custom in the summer, travelling alone he went to California to visit with friends and to minister with alumni of the Seminary. He reached Seattle and there, after an illness of about eight weeks, he died peacefully on August 22 in the home of his very dear friends, Mr. and Mrs. Robert O. Fleming. A long life of service had come to a close and the servant had gone into the presence of his waiting Lord.

Dallas, November 1953

# TABLES OF CONTENTS

# TABLE OF CONTENTS: VOLUME I

## PROLEGOMENA

CHAPTER I. PROLEGOMENA     3

  I. THE WORD *Theology*     3

  II. GENERAL USES OF THE WORD     4

     1. Natural Theology     4
     2. Revealed Theology     4
     3. Biblical Theology     4
     4. Theology Proper     5
     5. Historical Theology     5
     6. Dogmatic Theology     5
     7. Speculative Theology     5
     8. Old Testament Theology     5
     9. New Testament Theology     5
     10. Pauline, Johannine, Petrine Theologies     5
     11. Practical Theology     5
     12. Systematic or Thetic Theology     5

  III. VARIOUS DEFINITIONS     6

  IV. STUDENTS OF THEOLOGY     6

  V. ESSENTIAL REQUIREMENTS     7

     1. The Inspiration and Authority of the Scriptures Are Assumed     7
     2. The Laws of Methodology Are as Essential in the Science of Systematic Theology as in Any Other Science     7
     3. Finite Limitations Must Be Recognized     8
     4. Spiritual Illumination Is Necessary and Is Provided     9
     5. Patient and Tireless Study Is Required     10
     6. Faith     11
     7. Systematic Theology Should Be Unabridged     11

  VI. EXISTING ATTITUDES TOWARD THE SCRIPTURES     12

     1. Rationalism     12
       a. Extreme     12
       b. Moderate     12
     2. Mysticism     12
       a. False Mysticism     12
       b. True Mysticism     14

3. Romanism     14
4. The Orthodox Protestant Faith     15

VII. THE MAJOR DIVISIONS OF SYSTEMATIC THEOLOGY     15
1. Bibliology     15
2. Theology Proper     15
3. Angelology     15
4. Anthropology     16
5. Soteriology     16
6. Ecclesiology     16
7. Eschatology     16
8. Christology     16
9. Pneumatology     16
10. Doctrinal Summarization     16
CONCLUSION     16

## BIBLIOLOGY

CHAPTER II. INTRODUCTION TO BIBLIOLOGY     21

I. THE SUPERNATURAL ORIGIN OF THE BIBLE     22
1. The Book of God     23
2. The Bible and Monotheism     24
3. The Doctrine of the Trinity     24
    a. God the Father     25
    b. God the Son     25
    c. God the Spirit     25
4. Creation     26
5. Sin     26
6. The Cure of Evil according to the Bible     26
7. The Extent of Bible Revelation     27
8. The Ethics of the Bible     27
9. The Continuity of the Bible     29
10. Prophecy and Its Fulfillment     30
11. Types with Their Antitypes     31
12. The Bible as Literature     31
13. The Bible and Science     34
14. The Bible and Temporal Power     35
15. The Bible's Enduring Freshness     35

II. GENERAL DIVISIONS OF THE BIBLE     36
1. The Structure of the Bible     36
2. Created Beings and Their Relationships     37
    a. The Angels     37
    b. The Gentiles     37

c. The Jews    38
d. The Christians    38
3. The Time Periods of the Bible    40
   a. Divisions Related to Humanity    40
     (1) The First Period    40
     (2) The Second Period    40
     (3) The Third Period    40
     (4) The Fourth Period    40
   b. Dispensations    40
     (1) The Dispensation of Innocence    40
     (2) The Dispensation of Conscience    40
     (3) The Dispensation of Human Government    40
     (4) The Dispensation of Promise    41
     (5) The Dispensation of Law    41
     (6) The Dispensation of Grace    41
     (7) The Dispensation of Kingdom Rule    41
   c. The Covenants    41
     (1) The Covenant of Redemption    42
     (2) The Covenant of Works    42
     (3) The Covenant of Grace    42
     (4) The Edenic Covenant    42
     (5) The Adamic Covenant    42
     (6) The Noahic Covenant    42
     (7) The Abrahamic Covenant    42
     (8) The Mosaic Covenant    42
     (9) The Palestinian Covenant    43
     (10) The Davidic Covenant    43
     (11) The New Covenant for the Church    43
     (12) The New Covenant for Israel    43
   d. The Prophetic Periods    43
     (1) From Adam to Abraham    43
     (2) From Abraham to Moses    43
     (3) From Moses to Daniel    43
     (4) From Daniel to Christ    43
     (5) From the First to the Second Advent of Christ    44
     (6) From the Beginning to the End of the Millennial Kingdom    44
     (7) The Eternal State    44
   e. The Various Aspects of the Earthly Kingdom    44
     (1) The Theocracy    44
     (2) The Kingdom Promised    44
     (3) The Kingdom Anticipated by Prophets    44
     (4) The Kingdom Announced as "at Hand"    45
     (5) The Mystery Form of the Kingdom    45
     (6) The Kingdom to Be Reannounced by the 144,000 in Final Anticipation of the Messiah's Return    45
     (7) The Kingdom in Manifestation    45
   f. Divisions of the Scriptures Relative to the History of Israel in the Land    46

g. Divisions of the Scriptures Relative to the Gentiles 46
   (1) As outside the Jewish Covenants and Commonwealth Privileges 46
   (2) As Receiving a Dispensation of World Rule at the Hour of Israel's Last Dispersion 46
   (3) As Now Privileged to Receive the Gospel of Divine Grace 46
   (4) As Brought into Judgment at the End of Their Dispensation of World Rule 46
   (5) As Seen in Prophecy 46
   (6) As Entering and Continuing in Israel's Kingdom 46
   (7) As Partakers in the Glory of the Celestial City 46
h. Divisions of the Scriptures Relative to the Church 46
   (1) As Seen in Types 46
   (2) As Anticipated Directly in Prophecy 46
   (3) As Being Called out from, and Yet Resident in, the World 46
   (4) As Distinct from Judaism 47
   (5) As Caught up into Heaven by Resurrection and Translation 47
   (6) As Returning with Christ to His Earthly Reign 47
   (7) As Reigning with Christ on the Earth 47
   (8) As Partakers in the Glory of the New Heaven 47
4. Main Divisions of Bibliology 47

CHAPTER III.  REVELATION 48

I.  THREE IMPORTANT DOCTRINES DISTINGUISHED 48

1. Revelation and Reason 48
2. Revelation and Inspiration 49
3. Revelation, Inspiration, and Illumination 50

II.  THE NATURE OF REVELATION 51

1. God Revealed through Nature 53
2. God Revealed through Providence 54
3. God Revealed through Preservation 55
4. God Revealed through Miracles 56
5. God Revealed by Direct Communication 56
6. God Revealed through the Incarnation 58
7. God Revealed through the Scriptures 59
   a. Divine Revelation Is Varied in its Themes 60
   b. Divine Revelation Is Partial 60
   c. Concerning the Facts Revealed, Divine Revelation Is Complete 60
   d. Divine Revelation Is Progressive 60
   e. Divine Revelation Is Primarily unto Redemption 60

f. Divine Revelation Is Final          60
g. Divine Revelation Is Accurate to the Point of Infinity          60

Chapter IV. Inspiration          61

I. the fact and importance of inspiration          63

1. Christ versus the Apostles          64
2. Accommodation          65
3. Ignorance          65
4. Contradiction          66

II. theories of inspiration          68

1. The Mechanical or Dictation Theory          68
2. Partial Inspiration          68
3. Degrees of Inspiration          69
4. The Concept and Not the Words Inspired          69
5. Natural Inspiration          70
6. Mystical Inspiration          70
7. Verbal, Plenary Inspiration          71

III. dual authorship          72

IV. god's word about god's word          76

V. general objections to verbal, plenary inspiration          85

conclusion          88

Chapter V. Canonicity and Authority          89

I. the scriptures are authoritative being god-breathed          94

II. the scriptures are authoritative being written by chosen men who were "borne along" by the holy spirit          94

III. the scriptures are authoritative being accredited by those who first received them          95

IV. the scriptures are authoritative being attested by the lord jesus christ—the second person of the godhead          95

V. the scriptures are authoritative being received, delivered, and attested by the prophets          98

1. The Congregation's Relation to the Scriptures          98
2. The King's Relation to the Scriptures          98
3. The Officials' Relation to the Scriptures          98
4. The Levites' Relation to the Scriptures          99
5. The Prophets' Relation to the Scriptures          99

VI. the scriptures are authoritative being the word employed by god the holy spirit          102

VII.   THE AUTHORITY OF THE BIBLE IS SEEN IN THE FACT THAT
       WITHOUT THE SLIGHTEST DEFLECTION IT VINDICATES AND
       SATISFIES ITS EVERY CLAIM                                  102
       1. Enduring Power                                          102
       2. Imperial Power                                          102
       3. Sanctifying Power                                       103
       4. Revealing Power                                         103
       5. Accuracy                                                103
       6. Prevailing Power                                        103
       7. Prophecy                                                104
       CONCLUSION                                                 104

CHAPTER VI.   ILLUMINATION                                        105

   I.   SPECIFIC FORMS OF SPIRITUAL DARKNESS                      105
        1. Israel's Blindness                                     105
        2. Gentile Darkness                                       107
        3. Satanic Darkness                                       107
        4. Carnal Blindness                                       108

   II.  THE ILLUMINATING WORK OF THE SPIRIT                       109

CHAPTER VII.   INTERPRETATION                                     114

   I.    THE PURPOSE OF THE BIBLE AS A WHOLE                      115
   II.   THE DISTINCTIVE CHARACTER AND MESSAGE OF EACH BOOK OF
         THE BIBLE                                                116
   III.  TO WHOM IS A GIVEN SCRIPTURE ADDRESSED?                  116
   IV.   CONSIDERATION OF THE CONTEXT                             117
   V.    CONSIDERATION OF ALL SCRIPTURE BEARING ON ANY GIVEN THEME 117
   VI.   DISCOVERY OF THE EXACT MEANING OF THE DETERMINATIVE
         WORDS IN THE TEXT                                        118
   VII.  NECESSITY OF AVOIDING PERSONAL PREJUDICES                119

CHAPTER VIII.   ANIMATION                                         120

   I.   THE POWER OF GOD'S WORD UPON THE UNSAVED                  121
   II.  THE POWER OF GOD'S WORD UPON THE SAVED                    122

CHAPTER IX.   PRESERVATION                                        124

THEOLOGY PROPER

CHAPTER X.   INTRODUCTION TO THEOLOGY PROPER                      129

   I.   INTUITION                                                 130
   II.  TRADITION                                                 132

1. The Remote . . . . . . . . . . . . . . . . . . . . 132
2. The Present . . . . . . . . . . . . . . . . . . . 132

III. REASON . . . . . . . . . . . . . . . . . . . . . . . . 133

1. The Intrinsic Value . . . . . . . . . . . . . 133
2. The Achievements . . . . . . . . . . . . . . 134

IV. REVELATION . . . . . . . . . . . . . . . . . . . . 135

### NATURALISTIC THEISM

CHAPTER XI. NATURALISTIC THEISTIC ARGUMENTS . . . 137

I. THE COSMOLOGICAL ARGUMENT . . . . . . . 142

II. THE TELEOLOGICAL ARGUMENT . . . . . . . . 149

III. THE ANTHROPOLOGICAL ARGUMENT . . . . . 155

IV. THE ONTOLOGICAL ARGUMENT . . . . . . . . 158

CONCLUSION . . . . . . . . . . . . . . . . . . . . 161

CHAPTER XII. ANTITHEISTIC THEORIES . . . . . . . . . 162

I. ATHEISM . . . . . . . . . . . . . . . . . . . . . . . 163

II. AGNOSTICISM . . . . . . . . . . . . . . . . . . . 164

III. EVOLUTION . . . . . . . . . . . . . . . . . . . . . 166

IV. MATERIALISM . . . . . . . . . . . . . . . . . . . 171

V. POLYTHEISM . . . . . . . . . . . . . . . . . . . . 172

VI. IDEALISM AND REALISM . . . . . . . . . . . . 172

VII. PANTHEISM . . . . . . . . . . . . . . . . . . . . . 173

VIII. DEISM . . . . . . . . . . . . . . . . . . . . . . . . . 176

IX. POSITIVISM . . . . . . . . . . . . . . . . . . . . . 176

X. MONISM . . . . . . . . . . . . . . . . . . . . . . . 177

XI. DUALISM . . . . . . . . . . . . . . . . . . . . . . . 177

XII. PLURALISM . . . . . . . . . . . . . . . . . . . . . 178

CONCLUSION . . . . . . . . . . . . . . . . . . . . 178

### BIBLICAL THEISM

CHAPTER XIII. THE PERSONALITY OF GOD . . . . . . . 179

I. THE PERSONALITY OF GOD . . . . . . . . . . . 180

CHAPTER XIV. THE ATTRIBUTES OF GOD . . . . . . . . 187

I. PERSONALITY . . . . . . . . . . . . . . . . . . . 191

      1. Omniscience                                      192
      2. Sensibility                                      200
         a. Holiness                                   202
         b. Justice                                    203
         c. Love                                       205
         d. Goodness                                   206
         e. Truth                                      207
      3. Will                                             208
         a. Freedom                                    209
         b. Omnipotence                                209

II.   CONSTITUTIONAL ATTRIBUTES                            212

      1. Simplicity                                      213
      2. Unity                                           214
      3. Infinity                                        215
      4. Eternity                                        216
      5. Immutability                                    217
      6. Omnipresence or Immensity                       219
      7. Sovereignty                                     222
   CONCLUSION                                             223

CHAPTER XV.  DIVINE DECREES                               225

I.   THE DECREE OF GOD                                      228

      1. Two Basic Problems                              233
         a. The Moral Problem                          233
            (1) The Essential Nature of Sin         234
            (2) The Permission of Sin               236
         b. The Problem of the Will                    238
      2. Predestination                                  244
         a. Election                                   244
         b. Retribution                                246
      3. Objections to the Doctrine of Divine Decree     248
         a. The Justice of God                         249
         b. The Love of God                            249
         c. Predestination Predetermines that Men Shall Sin   249
         d. Predestination and the Means to Its Ends   250
         e. Predestination and Gospel Preaching        250
         f. Predestination and Fatalism                251
         g. Divine Decree and Human Suffering          251
      4. Major Manifestations of the Divine Decree       253
         a. Creation                                   253
         b. The Program of the Ages                    253
         c. Preservation                               255
         d. Providence                                 255
         e. Prayer                                     256
         f. Miracles                                   256
         g. Grace                                      257
   CONCLUSION                                             257

Chapter XVI.  The Names of Deity                                    260

   I.  the primary names of deity in the old testament       262
      1. Jehovah                                            262
      2. Elohim                                             264
      3. Adon, Adonai                                       268

  II.  compounds                                                269

 III.  old testament epithets                                    269

  IV.  new testament names of deity                            270

     conclusion                                            270

TRINITARIANISM

Chapter XVII.  Introduction to Trinitarianism                      272

   I.  preliminary consideration                           275

  II.  three dishonors                                         278
      1. Christ                                             278
      2. The Holy Spirit                                    280
      3. The Scriptures                                     281

 III.  general definition                                        282

  IV.  the true emphasis                                      286

Chapter XVIII.  Proof of the Trinitarian Doctrine                  289

   I.  reason                                              289
      1. The Divine Attributes Are Eternal                  291
      2. Eternal Activity of the Attributes                 291
      3. The Attributes Require Both Agent and Object       291
      4. God Is Sufficient in Himself                       293
      5. The Agent and Object Are Persons                   293
      6. Plurality in God Is a Trinity                      294
      7. The Bible Sustains Reason                          295
        a. The Eternal Exercise of Love                   296
        b. The Exercise of Mutual Glory                   296
        c. The Exercise of Knowing                        296
        d. The Exercise of Divine Disposition to Communion  297

  II.  revelation                                             297
      1. The Doctrine of the Trinity as Set Forth in the Old
        Testament                                         298
      2. The Doctrine of the Trinity as Set Forth in the New
        Testament                                         302
        a. The Trinity and the Names of God               303
        b. The Trinity and the Attributes of God          304

c. The Trinity and the Works of God          305
    (1) Creation of the Universe          305
    (2) Creation of Man          306
    (3) The Incarnation          306
    (4) The Life and Ministry of Christ          306
    (5) The Death of Christ          306
    (6) The Resurrection of Christ          307
    (7) The Resurrection of All Mankind          307
    (8) The Inspiration of the Scriptures          307
    (9) The Minister's Authority          307
    (10) The Indwelling Presence          307
    (11) The Work of Sanctification          308
    (12) The Believer's Safekeeping          308
d. The Trinity and the Worship of God          308
    (1) By Angels          308
    (2) By Saints          308
    (3) The Benedictions          308

CHAPTER XIX.  GOD THE FATHER          311

    I.   FATHERHOOD OVER CREATION          312

    II.  FATHERHOOD BY INTIMATE RELATIONSHIP          313

    III. THE FATHER OF OUR LORD JESUS CHRIST          313

    IV.  FATHERHOOD OVER ALL WHO BELIEVE          316

CHAPTER XX.  GOD THE SON: HIS PREEXISTENCE          318

    I.   MAJOR PASSAGES ON PREEXISTENCE          322

    II.  THE ANGEL OF JEHOVAH          327

        1. A Divine Person          327
        2. Part of the Trinity          329

CHAPTER XXI.  GOD THE SON: HIS NAMES          332

    I.   JEHOVAH, LORD          332

    II.  ELOHIM, GOD          334

    III. SON OF GOD, SON OF MAN          335

    IV.  LORD JESUS CHRIST          337

CHAPTER XXII.  GOD THE SON: HIS DEITY          339

    I.   DIVINE ATTRIBUTES BELONG TO CHRIST          340

        1. Eternity          340
        2. Immutability          341
        3. Omnipotence          341
        4. Omniscience          341
        5. Omnipresence          341
        6. Other Major Attributes          342

II.  THE PREROGATIVES OF DEITY ARE ASCRIBED TO CHRIST        342

    1. He Is Creator of All Things                              342
    2. He Is Preserver of All Things                            343
    3. He Pardons Sin                                           343
    4. Christ Will Raise the Dead                               343
    5. Christ Apportions the Rewards of Saints                  343
    6. The Judgment of the World Is Committed to Christ         343
    7. That Worship Which Belongs Only to God Is Freely
       Rendered to Christ                                344
    OBJECTIONS                                                 345

CHAPTER XXIII.  GOD THE SON: HIS INCARNATION                 348

  I.  WHO BECAME INCARNATE?                                   349

  II.  HOW DID THE SON BECOME INCARNATE?                      354

  III.  FOR WHAT PURPOSE DID HE BECOME INCARNATE?            355

    1. That He Might Manifest God to Man                        355
    2. That He Might Manifest Man to God                        357
    3. That He Might Be a Merciful and Faithful High Priest     357
    4. That He Might Destroy the Works of the Devil             358
    5. That He Might Be Head over the New Creation              358
    6. That He Might Sit on David's Throne                      359
    7. That He Might Be a Kinsman Redeemer                      361
    CONCLUSION                                                 364

CHAPTER XXIV.  GOD THE SON: HIS HUMANITY                     365

  I.  CHRIST'S HUMANITY WAS ANTICIPATED BEFORE THE FOUNDA-
      TION OF THE WORLD                                    367

  II.  THE OLD TESTAMENT EXPECTATION WAS OF A HUMAN MESSIAH     367

    1. The Types                                               367
    2. Prophecy                                                367

  III.  A SPECIFIC NEW TESTAMENT PROPHECY                     368

  IV.  THE LIFE OF CHRIST ON EARTH                            368

    1. His Names                                               368
    2. His Human Parentage                                      368
    3. The Fact That He Possessed a Human Body, Soul, and
       Spirit                                            369
    4. His Human Limitations                                    369

  V.  THE DEATH AND RESURRECTION OF CHRIST                    370

  VI.  THE HUMANITY OF CHRIST IS SEEN IN HIS ASCENSION AND
      SESSION                                              370

VII.   THE HUMANITY OF CHRIST IS EVIDENT IN HIS SECOND ADVENT
       AND KINGDOM REIGN                                          370

       CONCLUSION                                                 371

CHAPTER XXV.   GOD THE SON: THE KENOSIS                           373

    I.   "THE FORM OF GOD"                                        375

   II.   THE CONDESCENSION                                        377

  III.   "THE FORM OF A SERVANT. . .THE LIKENESS OF MEN"          378
         CONCLUSION                                               381

CHAPTER XXVI.   GOD THE SON: THE HYPOSTATIC UNION                 382

    I.   THE STRUCTURE OF THE DOCTRINE                            383
         1. His Deity                                             383
         2. His Humanity                                          383
         3. The Complete Preservation of Each of His Two Natures
            without Confusion or Alteration of Them and Their
            Unity                                                 384

   II.   THE RELATIONSHIPS                                        389
         1. To the Father                                         389
         2. To the Spirit                                         390
         3. To Himself                                            390
         4. To Angels Unfallen and Fallen                         392
         5. To Humanity                                           392
         6. To Sin and the Sin Nature                             393
            a. The Impeccability of Christ                        393
         7. To Those Who Are Saved                                395
         CONCLUSION                                               395

CHAPTER XXVII.   GOD THE HOLY SPIRIT                              397

    I.   THE PERSONALITY OF THE HOLY SPIRIT                       397

   II.   THE DEITY OF THE HOLY SPIRIT                             399
         1. The Holy Spirit Is Called God                         399
         2. The Holy Spirit Is Associated with God                399
         3. The Attributes of God Are Predicated of the Holy Spirit 401
         4. The Holy Spirit May Be Blasphemed                     401

  III.   THE WITNESS OF THE OLD TESTAMENT                         402
         1. The Holy Spirit in Cosmical Undertakings              403
         2. The Holy Spirit's Work in Things Governmental         404
         3. The Holy Spirit in Relation to Individuals            407

   IV.   THE WITNESS OF THE NEW TESTAMENT                         410

# TABLE OF CONTENTS: VOLUME II

## ANGELOLOGY

CHAPTER I.   INTRODUCTION TO ANGELOLOGY                                    3

CHAPTER II.   GENERAL FACTS ABOUT THE ANGELS                              6

   I.   ANGELIC SPHERES                                              6

  II.   THE REALITY OF THE ANGELS                                      8

 III.   RELATIVE IMPORTANCE OF ANGELS AND MEN                           9

 IV.   THE PERSONALITY OF THE ANGELS                                   10

  V.   THE CREATION AND MODE OF EXISTENCE OF THE ANGELS            11

 VI.   THE ABODE OF THE ANGELS                                         14

VII.   THE NUMBER OF THE ANGELS                                          15

VIII.   THE POWER OF THE ANGELS                                          15

 IX.   THE CLASSIFICATION OF THE ANGELS                               16

     1. Governmental Rulers                                16

     2. Elect Angels                                      17

     3. Cherubim, Seraphim, and Living Creatures          17

       a. Cherubim                                   17

       b. Seraphim                                   18

       c. Living Creatures                           19

     4. Individual Angels                                 19

       a. Lucifer, Son of the Morning (Isa. 14:12)   19

       b. Michael (Dan. 12:1)                        19

       c. Gabriel (Dan. 9:21)                        20

     5. Angels Especially Designated                      20

  X.   THE MINISTRY OF THE ANGELS                                   21

 XI.   THE PROGRESSIVE DISCIPLINE OF THE ANGELS                        24

XII.   THE ANGELS AS SPECTATORS                                          26

     CONCLUSION                                           27

CHAPTER III.   ANGELIC PARTICIPATION IN THE MORAL PROBLEM                 28

CHAPTER IV.   SATANOLOGY: INTRODUCTION                                    33

CHAPTER V.   SATANOLOGY: THE CAREER OF SATAN                              39

Table of Contents: Volume II      23

I.    SATAN'S CREATION, ORIGINAL ESTATE, AND FALL    39

II.    SATAN'S SIN    44

     1. "I Will Ascend into Heaven"    48
     2. "I Will Exalt My Throne above the Stars of God"    48
     3. "I Will Sit Also upon the Mount of the Congregation, in the Sides of the North"    48
     4. "I Will Ascend above the Heights of the Clouds"    49
     5. "I Will Be Like the Most High"    49

III.    SATAN ACCORDING TO THE OLD TESTAMENT    50

IV.    SATAN ACCORDING TO THE NEW TESTAMENT    51

V.    SATAN JUDGED IN THE CROSS    53

VI.    THE EXECUTION OF SATAN'S JUDGMENTS    57

     1. Satan Cast out of Heaven    58
     2. Satan's Judgment at the Second Advent of Christ    60
     3. Satan's Final Judgment    61

CHAPTER VI.   SATANOLOGY: SATAN'S EVIL CHARACTER    62

I.    TWOFOLD WICKEDNESS    63

     1. Ambitious Pride    63
     2. Untruth    64
        a. Three Forces    70
           (1) The Force of the Man of Sin    70
           (2) The Force of the Restrainer    71
           (3) The Force of the Destroyer    71

II.    SATAN'S SINFULNESS    72

CHAPTER VII.   SATANOLOGY: THE SATANIC *Cosmos*    76

I.    SATAN'S AUTHORITY OVER THE *Cosmos*    80

II.    THE *Cosmos* IS WHOLLY EVIL    84

III.    SATAN'S UNDERTAKINGS IN THE *Cosmos*    86

IV.    THE THINGS OF THE *Cosmos*    87

V.    THOUGH DETAINED HERE, CHRISTIANS ARE NOT OF THE *Cosmos*    87

VI.    THE IMPOTENCY OF THE *Cosmos*    88

VII.    THE END OF THE *Cosmos*    89

CHAPTER VIII.   SATANOLOGY: SATAN'S MOTIVE    91

CHAPTER IX.   SATANOLOGY: SATAN'S METHOD    99

   CONCLUSION TO SATANOLOGY    111

CHAPTER X.   DEMONOLOGY    113

## ANTHROPOLOGY

CHAPTER XI. INTRODUCTION TO ANTHROPOLOGY 125

CHAPTER XII. THE ORIGIN OF MAN 130

    I. THE EVOLUTIONARY THEORY 130

    II. REVELATION 135

    III. THE TIME OF MAN'S ORIGIN 138

CHAPTER XIII. THE MATERIAL PART OF MAN AT CREATION 144

    I. THE STRUCTURAL CHARACTER OF THE HUMAN BODY 145

    II. THE FUTURE OF THE HUMAN BODY 149

    III. VARIOUS USES OF THE WORD *Body* 157

    IV. THE BODY OF CHRIST 158

    CONCLUSION 159

CHAPTER XIV. THE IMMATERIAL PART OF MAN AT CREATION 160

    I. THE ORIGIN OF THE IMMATERIAL PART OF THE FIRST MAN 160

    II. THE DIVINE IMAGE 161

    III. THE DERIVATION AND PERPETUATION OF THE IMMATERIAL PART OF MAN 173

        1. The Pre-Existence Theory 173

        2. The Creation Theory 174

        3. The Traducian Theory 177

    IV. ELEMENTS WHICH COMPRISE THE IMMATERIAL PART OF MAN 180

        1. Soul 182

        2. Spirit 184

        3. Heart 187

        4. Flesh 188

        5. Mind 191

    V. THE CAPACITIES AND FACULTIES OF THE IMMATERIAL PART OF MAN 192

        1. Intellect 193

        2. Sensibility 194

        3. Will 194

        4. Conscience 197

CHAPTER XV. THE STATE OF INNOCENCE 200

    I. THE ENVIRONMENT OF THE FIRST MAN 200

II.　THE RESPONSIBILITY OF THE FIRST MAN　　202

III.　THE MORAL QUALITIES OF THE FIRST MAN　　202

IV.　THE TEMPTER OF THE FIRST MAN　　203

V.　THE TEMPTATION OF THE FIRST MAN　　209

CHAPTER XVI.　THE FALL　　215

　I.　SPIRITUAL DEATH AND DEPRAVITY　　217

　II.　PHYSICAL DEATH　　222

　　CONCLUSION　　223

CHAPTER XVII.　INTRODUCTION TO HAMARTIOLOGY　　224

　I.　THE ESSENTIAL NATURE OF SIN　　227

　II.　THE DERIVATION OF SIN　　228

　III.　THE DIVINE PERMISSION OF SIN　　229

　　1. The Divine Recognition of the Creature's Free Choice　　231
　　2. The Specific Value of Redeemed Beings　　231
　　3. The Acquisition of Divine Knowledge　　231
　　4. The Instruction of Angels　　232
　　5. The Demonstration of the Divine Hatred of Evil　　232
　　6. The Righteous Judgments of All Evil　　232
　　7. The Manifestation and Exercise of Divine Grace　　232

　　PREPARATORY REMARKS　　233

CHAPTER XVIII.　PERSONAL SIN　　235

　I.　THE ORIGIN OF SIN　　235

　　1. The Eternal Anticipation of Sin in the Foreknowledge of
　　　God　　236
　　2. The First Concrete Enactment of Sin in Heaven by an
　　　Unfallen Angel　　242
　　　a. The Person Who First Sinned　　243
　　　b. The Nature of the First Sin　　246
　　3. The First Concrete Enactment of Sin by a Human Being
　　　on Earth　　248

　II.　THE SINFUL NATURE OF SIN　　251

　III.　THREE MAJOR PROOFS OF THE EXCEEDING SINFULNESS OF
　　　PERSONAL SIN　　252

　　1. The Angelic Proof　　252
　　2. The Human Proof　　252
　　3. The Divine Proof　　252

IV. GENERAL DEFINITIONS . . . . . . . . . . . . 254

    1. Sin against God's Holy Person . . . . . . . . 255
        a. The Theory That Sin Is Selfishness . . . . 258
    2. Sin against the Law . . . . . . . . . . . . 260
        a. Early Communications Preserved by Tradition . . 260
        b. Human Conscience . . . . . . . . . . . 261
        c. Direct Spiritual Guidance . . . . . . . . 262
        d. The Written Word of God with its Various Age-
           Applications . . . . . . . . . . . . . 262

V. GENERAL TERMS AND CLASSIFICATIONS . . . . . . 267

VI. THE DIVINE REMEDY FOR PERSONAL SIN . . . . . 269

    1. Forgiveness . . . . . . . . . . . . . . . 270
    2. Justification . . . . . . . . . . . . . . . 273

VII. ORIGINAL SIN . . . . . . . . . . . . . . . . 278

VIII. GUILT . . . . . . . . . . . . . . . . . . . 279

IX. UNIVERSALITY . . . . . . . . . . . . . . . . 281

CHAPTER XIX. THE TRANSMITTED SIN NATURE . . . . . 283

I. THE FACT OF THE SIN NATURE . . . . . . . . . 285

II. THE REMEDY FOR THE SIN NATURE . . . . . . . 292

CHAPTER XX. IMPUTED SIN . . . . . . . . . . . . 296

I. THE SCOPE OF THE DOCTRINE OF IMPUTATION . . 297

II. THEORIES OF IMPUTATION . . . . . . . . . . 310

III. THE DIVINE REMEDY FOR IMPUTED SIN . . . . . 312

    1. The Death of Christ . . . . . . . . . . . 313
    2. The Keys of Death . . . . . . . . . . . . 314
    3. Death and the Unsaved . . . . . . . . . . 314
    4. Death and the Christian . . . . . . . . . . 314
    5. Death in the Millennium . . . . . . . . . . 314

    CONCLUSION . . . . . . . . . . . . . . . . 315

CHAPTER XXI. MAN'S ESTATE UNDER SIN AND HIS RELATION TO
SATAN . . . . . . . . . . . . . . . . . . . . 316

I. THE FACT . . . . . . . . . . . . . . . . . 316

II. THE REMEDY . . . . . . . . . . . . . . . . 319

III. THE RELATION OF THE UNSAVED TO SATAN . . . . 323

CHAPTER XXII. THE CHRISTIAN'S SIN AND ITS REMEDY . . 325

I. THE WORLD . . . . . . . . . . . . . . . . 330

II. THE FLESH     330

III. THE DEVIL     331

IV. THE THREEFOLD PROVISION     332
     1. The Word of God     333
     2. The Interceding Christ     333
     3. The Indwelling Spirit     333

V. THE TWOFOLD EFFECT OF THE CHRISTIAN'S SIN     334
     1. The Effect of the Christian's Sin upon Himself     334
     2. The Effect of the Christian's Sin upon God     342

VI. THE CHRISTIAN'S SIN NATURE     345
     1. "Flesh"     346
     2. "Old Man"     347
     3. "Sin"     348
         a. The Divine Provision     349
         b. The Believer's Responsibility     353

VII. THE CHRISTIAN'S RELATION TO IMPUTED SIN     358

VIII. THE CHRISTIAN'S RELATION TO MAN'S ESTATE UNDER SIN     358

CHAPTER XXIII. PUNISHMENT     360

I. CHASTISEMENT     360

II. SCOURGING     361

III. RETRIBUTION     361

CHAPTER XXIV. THE FINAL TRIUMPH OVER ALL SIN     365

# TABLE OF CONTENTS: VOLUME III

## SOTERIOLOGY

CHAPTER I. INTRODUCTION TO SOTERIOLOGY                    3

### THE SAVIOR

CHAPTER II. THE PERSON OF THE SAVIOR                      11

  I. CHRIST'S SEVEN POSITIONS                            12

    1. The Preincarnate Christ                      12
    2. The Incarnate Christ                         15
    3. Christ in His Death                          15
    4. The Resurrected Christ                       16
    5. Christ Ascended and Seated in Heaven         16
    6. Christ Returning                             16
    7. Christ Reigning Forever                      17

  II. CHRIST'S OFFICES                                  17

    1. Prophet                                      17
      a. The Preincarnate Ministry                21
      b. The Incarnate Ministry                   21
        (1) Six Features of Christ's Incarnate Ministry  21
          (a) "God Was Manifest in the Flesh"  21
          (b) "Justified in the Spirit"        22
          (c) "Seen of Angels"                 22
          (d) "Preached unto the Gentiles"     22
          (e) "Believed on in the World"       22
          (f) "Received up into Glory"         23
        (2) Christ Forthtelling and Foretelling  23
          (a) Christ Forthtelling              23
          (b) Christ Foretelling               25
      c. The Ministry from Heaven                 26
    2. Priest                                       26
      a. In His Person                            27
      b. By Appointment                           29
      c. Eternal Duration                         29
    3. King                                         30

  III. THE SONSHIPS OF CHRIST                          30

    1. The Son of God                               30
    2. The Son of Man                               31
    3. The Son of David                             33

4. The Son of Abraham ........................................ 33

IV. THE HYPOSTATIC UNION ........................................ 33

CONCLUSION ........................................ 34

Chapter III. Introduction to the Sufferings of Christ        35

I. SUFFERINGS IN LIFE ........................................ 36

1. Sufferings Due to His Holy Character ................ 37
2. Sufferings Due to Christ's Compassion ............... 38
3. Sufferings Due to Anticipation ...................... 39

II. SUFFERINGS IN DEATH ........................................ 43

1. Contrast between the Crucifixion and the Cross ...... 44
2. Who Put Christ to Death? ............................ 49
3. What Christ Suffered at the Hands of Men and What He
   Suffered at the Hands of His Father ................. 51
4. The Value of Christ's Sufferings to the Father ...... 51
5. The Wisdom, Power, and Sacrifice of God ............. 52
6. The Unified Action of the Three Persons ............. 53
7. Two Major Features of Soteriology .................. 54

Chapter IV. Things Accomplished by Christ in His Sufferings
            and Death        55

I. A SUBSTITUTION FOR SINNERS ................................. 55

1. The Words Which Imply Substitution ................. 56
2. Vicarious Suffering in General ..................... 57
3. Mediation ......................................... 61
4. Substitution with Respect to the Judgment of Sin .. 62
5. Substitution in the Realms of Divine Perfection ... 72

II. CHRIST THE ENDING OF THE LAW PRINCIPLE IN BEHALF OF
    THOSE WHO ARE SAVED        76

III. A REDEMPTION TOWARD SIN .................................. 86

IV. A RECONCILIATION TOWARD MAN ............................... 91

V. A PROPITIATION TOWARD GOD .................................. 93

VI. THE JUDGMENT OF THE SIN NATURE ............................ 96

VII. THE GROUND OF THE BELIEVER'S FORGIVENESS AND CLEANSING 101

VIII. THE GROUND FOR THE DEFERRING OF RIGHTEOUS DIVINE JUDG-
      MENTS        102

IX. THE TAKING AWAY OF PRECROSS SIN ONCE COVERED BY SACRIFICE 103

X. THE NATIONAL SALVATION OF ISRAEL .......................... 105

XI. MILLENNIAL AND ETERNAL BLESSINGS UPON GENTILES .......... 108

XII.   THE SPOILING OF PRINCIPALITIES AND POWERS                      109

XIII.   THE GROUND OF PEACE                                           112

XIV.   THE PURIFICATION OF THINGS IN HEAVEN                           113

CHAPTER V.   THE SUFFERINGS AND DEATH OF CHRIST IN TYPES              116

    I.   THE GENERAL SACRIFICES OF THE OLD TESTAMENT              119

        1. Abel's Offering                                    119
        2. Noah's Altar and Sacrifice                        119

    II.   THE PRESCRIBED SACRIFICES OF THE OLD TESTAMENT           120

        1. The Paschal Lamb                                   120
        2. The Five Offerings (Lev. 1:1—7:38)                121
        3. The Two Birds (Lev. 14:1–7)                       122
        4. The Day of Atonement                               122
        5. The Red Heifer (Num. 19:1–22)                     123

    III.   MISCELLANEOUS TYPES OF CHRIST'S DEATH                   124

        1. The Coats of Skin (Gen. 3:21)                     124
        2. Noah's Ark (Gen. 6:14—8:19)                       124
        3. Bread and Wine at the Hand of Melchizedek (Gen.
           14:17–24)                                        124
        4. The Offering of Isaac (Gen. 22:1–14)              124
        5. Joseph (Gen. 37:2—50:26)                          124
        6. Manna in the Wilderness (Ex. 16:14–22)            125
        7. The Smitten Rock (Ex. 17:5–7; Num. 20:7–13)      125
        8. The Tabernacle (Ex. 25:1—40:38)                  125

    IV.   THE DEATH OF CHRIST ACCORDING TO VARIOUS SCRIPTURES    125

        1. The Death of Christ according to Genesis          125
        2. The Death of Christ according to Old Testament
           Prophecy                                          126
        3. The Death of Christ according to the Gospels      126
        4. The Death of Christ according to Romans, 1 and 2
           Corinthians, and Galatians                        126
        5. The Death of Christ according to Ephesians, Philippians,
           and Colossians                                    126
        6. The Death of Christ according to the Epistle to the
           Hebrews                                           126
        7. The Death of Christ according to Other Books of the
           New Testament                                     126

CHAPTER VI.   BIBLICAL TERMINOLOGY RELATED TO CHRIST'S SUFFER-
               INGS AND DEATH                                     127

    I.   ATONEMENT                                                127

    II.   EXPIATION                                               127

III. FORGIVENESS AND REMISSION          128

IV. GUILT          128

V. JUSTICE          128

VI. JUSTIFICATION          128

VII. PENALTY          128

VIII. PROPITIATION          129

IX. RECONCILIATION          129

X. REDEMPTION AND RANSOM          129

XI. SACRIFICE          129

XII. SATISFACTION          129

XIII. VICARIOUS AND SUBSTITUTIONARY          130

CHAPTER VII. THEORIES FALSE AND TRUE OF THE VALUE OF CHRIST'S DEATH          131

I. PRELIMINARY CONSIDERATIONS          131
  1. General Facts Revealed          131
  2. The Death of Christ Is Unique          133
  3. Its Extent          134
  4. Its Three Directions          134
  5. Divine Satisfaction through Christ's Death Is Not Personal Salvation          134
  6. Type and Antitype          135
  7. Theories May Be Questioned          135

II. HISTORICAL RECORD          135
  1. From the Beginning to Anselm          135
  2. From Anselm to Grotius          137
  3. From Grotius to the Present Time          139

III. THEORIES IN GENERAL          139
  1. The Marturial Theory          141
  2. The Moral Influence Theory          141
  3. The Identification Theory          142
  4. The Rectoral or Governmental Theory          142
  5. The Doctrine of Satisfaction          154

  CONCLUSION          155

DIVINE ELECTION

CHAPTER VIII. THE FACT OF DIVINE ELECTION          165

I. THE TERMS USED          167

1. Biblical Usage 167
2. Chosen 168
3. Drawing 168
4. Calling 168
5. Divine Purpose 168
6. Foreknowledge 168
7. Foreordination and Predestination 168

II. A CLEAR REVELATION 168

III. ESSENTIAL TRUTHS EMBRACED 172

1. God Has by Election Chosen Some to Salvation, But Not All 172
2. Divine Election Was Accomplished in Eternity Past 172
3. Election Does Not Rest Merely on Foreknowledge 173
4. Divine Election Is Immutable 174
5. Election in Relation to Christ's Mediation 175

IV. OBJECTIONS TO THE DOCTRINE OF ELECTION 176

CHAPTER IX. THE ORDER OF ELECTIVE DECREES 178

I. THE ORDER SET FORTH BY THE SUPRALAPSARIANS 179

II. THE ORDER SET FORTH BY THE INFRALAPSARIANS 180

III. THE ORDER SET FORTH BY THE SUBLAPSARIANS 181

IV. THE ORDER SET FORTH BY THE ARMINIANS 182

CONCLUSION 182

CHAPTER X. FOR WHOM DID CHRIST DIE? 183

I. CLASSIFICATION OF VIEWS 184

1. The Extreme Limited Redemptionists 184
2. The Moderate Calvinists Who Are Limited Redemptionists 184
3. The Moderate Calvinists Who Are Unlimited Redemptionists 184
4. The Arminians 185

II. POINTS OF AGREEMENT AND DISAGREEMENT BETWEEN THE TWO SCHOOLS OF MODERATE CALVINISTS 185

III. DISPENSATIONAL ASPECTS OF THE PROBLEM 188

IV. THREE DOCTRINAL WORDS 190

V. THE CROSS IS NOT THE ONLY SAVING INSTRUMENTALITY 193

VI. UNIVERSAL GOSPEL PREACHING 194

VII. IS GOD DEFEATED IF MEN ARE LOST FOR WHOM CHRIST DIED? 195

VIII.   THE NATURE OF SUBSTITUTION                                      199

  IX.   THE TESTIMONY OF THE SCRIPTURES                                 201

      1. Passages Which Declare Christ's Death to Be for the
          Whole World (John 3:16; 2 Cor. 5:19; Heb. 2:9;
          1 John 2:2)                                                   203
      2. Passages Which Are All-Inclusive in Their Scope (2 Cor.
          5:14; 1 Tim. 2:6; 4:10; Titus 2:11; Rom. 5:6)                 204
      3. Passages Which Offer a Universal Gospel to Men (John
          3:16; Acts 10:43; Rev. 22:17, etc.)                          204
      4. A Special Passage: 2 Peter 2:1                                 204

      CONCLUSION                                                        205

THE SAVING WORK OF THE TRIUNE GOD

CHAPTER XI.   THE FINISHED WORK OF CHRIST                               206

CHAPTER XII.   THE CONVICTING WORK OF THE SPIRIT                        210

   I.   THE NEED OF THE SPIRIT'S WORK                                   211

  II.   THE FACT OF THE SPIRIT'S WORK                                   217
      1. "Of Sin"                                                       218
      2. "Of Righteousness"                                            219
      3. "Of Judgment"                                                  22C

 III.   THE RESULTS OF THE SPIRIT'S WORK                                223

CHAPTER XIII.   THE RICHES OF DIVINE GRACE                             225

   I.   THE ESTATE OF THE LOST                                          230

  II.   THE ESSENTIAL CHARACTER OF GOD'S UNDERTAKINGS                  232
      1. They Are Not Experienced                                      232
      2. They Are Not Progressive                                      233
      3. They Are Not Related to Human Merit                           233
      4. They Are Eternal in Their Character                           233
      5. They Are Known Only by Revelation                             233
      6. They Are Wrought by God Alone                                 234
      7. They Are Not Wrought by Man                                   234

 III.   THE RICHES OF DIVINE GRACE                                      234
      1. In the Eternal Plan of God                                    234
      2. Redeemed                                                       236
      3. Reconciled                                                     237
      4. Related to God through Propitiation                           237
      5. Forgiven All Trespasses                                       238
      6. Vitally Conjoined to Christ for the Judgment of the Old
          Man "unto a New Walk"                                        239

7. Free from the Law                                      240

8. Children of God                                        241

9. Adopted                                                242

10. Acceptable to God by Jesus Christ                     243
    a. Made Righteous                                     243
    b. Sanctified Positionally                            244
    c. Perfected Forever                                  245
    d. Made Accepted in the Beloved                       245
    e. Made Meet                                          245

11. Justified                                             245

12. Made Nigh                                             246

13. Delivered from the Power of Darkness                  247

14. Translated into the Kingdom of the Son of His Love    248

15. On the Rock, Christ Jesus                             248

16. A Gift from God the Father to Christ                  249

17. Circumcised in Christ                                 250

18. Partakers of the Holy and Royal Priesthood            251

19. A Chosen Generation, a Holy Nation, a Peculiar People 251

20. Heavenly Citizens                                     252

21. Of the Family and Household of God                    252

22. In the Fellowship of the Saints                       253

23. A Heavenly Association                                254
    a. Partners with Christ in Life                       255
    b. Partnership in Position                            255
    c. Partners with Christ in Service                    255
    d. Partners with Christ in Suffering                  256
    e. Partners with Christ in Prayer                     257
    f. Partners with Christ in Betrothal                  257
    g. Partners in Expectation                            257

24. Having Access to God                                  257
    a. Access into His Grace                              258
    b. Access unto the Father                             258
    c. Access Is Reassuring                               258

25. Within the Much More Care of God                      259
    a. Objects of His Love                                259
    b. Objects of His Grace                               259
        (1) Salvation                                     259
        (2) Safekeeping                                   259
        (3) Service                                       259
        (4) Instruction                                   260
    c. Objects of His Power                               260
    d. Objects of His Faithfulness                        260
    e. Objects of His Peace                               260
    f. Objects of His Consolation                         260
    g. Objects of His Intercession                        260

26. His Inheritance                                       261

27. The Inheritance of the Saints                         261

28. Light in the Lord                                     262

29. Vitally United to the Father, the Son, and the Holy
    Spirit                                                        262
30. Blessed with the Earnest or First-Fruits of the Spirit       263
31. Glorified                                                    264
32. Complete in Him                                              264
33. Possessing Every Spiritual Blessing                          265

   Conclusion                                                    265

THE ETERNAL SECURITY OF THE BELIEVER

Chapter XIV.  Introduction to the Doctrine of Security          267

Chapter XV.  The Arminian View of Security                      273

   I.  The Arminian View of Major Soteriological Doctrines       275
       1. The Arminian View of Original Sin                      275
       2. The Arminian View of Universal and Efficacious Calling 276
       3. The Arminian View of Divine Decrees                    278
       4. The Arminian View of the Fall                          279
       5. The Arminian View of Omniscience                       280
       6. The Arminian View of Divine Sovereignty                281
       7. The Arminian View of Sovereign Grace                   282

   II.  The Arminian Emphasis Upon Human Experience and
        Reason                                                   286

   III.  The Arminian Appeal to the Scriptures                   290
       1. Scriptures Dispensationally Misapplied                 292
       2. Passages Related to the False Teachers of the Last Days 293
       3. A Mere Reformation or Outward Profession               295
       4. A True Salvation Is Proved by Its Fruits               297
       5. Warnings to the Jews                                   302
       6. Warnings to All Men                                    305
       7. Gentiles May Be Broken Off Corporately                 306
       8. Believers May Lose Their Rewards and Be Disapproved    307
       9. Believers May Experience Loss of Fellowship            309
       10. Christians May Fall from Grace                        310
       11. Miscellaneous Passages                                311

   Conclusion                                                    312

Chapter XVI.  The Calvinistic Doctrine of Security              313

   I.  The Reasons Which Depend on God the Father                316
       1. The Sovereign Purpose of God                           316
       2. The Father's Infinite Power Set Free                   320

3. The Infinite Love of God — 321

4. The Influence on the Father of the Prayer of His Son — 323

II. THE REASONS WHICH DEPEND ON GOD THE SON — 324

1. Christ Has Died — 326

2. Christ Is Risen — 327

3. Christ Advocates — 328

4. Christ Intercedes — 331

III. RESPONSIBILITIES BELONGING TO GOD THE HOLY SPIRIT — 334

1. The Holy Spirit Regenerates — 335

2. The Holy Spirit Indwells — 336

3. The Holy Spirit Baptizes — 337

4. The Holy Spirit Seals — 338

CHAPTER XVII. THE CONSUMMATING SCRIPTURE — 340

I. DELIVERED FROM THE LAW — 342

II. THE FACT OF THE PRESENCE OF THE DIVINE NATURE — 345

III. THE CHRISTIAN A SON AND HEIR OF GOD — 346

IV. THE DIVINE PURPOSE — 347

V. THE EXECUTION OF THE DIVINE PURPOSE — 349

VI. CHRIST'S OWN ACHIEVEMENT — 351

VII. THE INCOMPETENCY OF CELESTIAL AND MUNDANE THINGS — 351

CONCLUSION — 354

CHAPTER XVIII. DELIVERANCE FROM THE REIGNING POWER OF SIN AND HUMAN LIMITATIONS — 355

I. DELIVERANCE FROM THE POWER OF SIN — 355

1. The World — 358

2. The Flesh — 359

3. The Devil — 359

CONCLUSION — 360

II. SALVATION FROM HUMAN LIMITATIONS — 361

1. The Spirit Produces Christian Character — 361

2. The Spirit Empowers unto Christian Service — 362

CONCLUSION — 363

CHAPTER XIX. THE BELIEVER PRESENTED FAULTLESS — 364

I. HEAVENLY CITIZENSHIP — 365

II. A NEW FRATERNITY — 365

III. A STANDING PERFECTED FOREVER 365

IV. A RENEWED BODY 366

V. FREEDOM FROM THE SIN NATURE 366

VI. TO BE LIKE CHRIST 367

VII. TO SHARE IN CHRIST'S GLORY 367

CONCLUSION 369

## THE TERMS OF SALVATION

CHAPTER XX. THE TERMS OF SALVATION 371

I. REPENT AND BELIEVE 372

1. The Meaning of the Word 372
2. The Relation of Repentance to Believing 373
3. The Relation of Repentance to Covenant People 375
4. The Absence of the Demand for Repentance from Salvation Scriptures 376
5. The Significance of Repentance in Specific Passages 377

CONCLUSION 378

II. BELIEVE AND CONFESS CHRIST 378

1. Scripture Bearing on Confession of Christ 379
2. Two Conclusive Reasons 380

CONCLUSION 380

III. BELIEVE AND BE BAPTIZED 381

CONCLUSION 384

IV. BELIEVE AND SURRENDER TO GOD 384

1. The Incapacity of the Unsaved 385
2. What Is Involved 386
3. The Preacher's Responsibility 386

CONCLUSION 387

V. BELIEVE AND CONFESS SIN OR MAKE RESTITUTION 388

VI. BELIEVE AND IMPLORE GOD TO SAVE 389

1. "Seek Ye the Lord" 389
2. Believe and Pray 389

EPILOGUE 394

# TABLE OF CONTENTS: VOLUME IV

## ECCLESIOLOGY

CHAPTER I. INTRODUCTION TO ECCLESIOLOGY     3

I. THE CREATURES OF GOD VIEWED DISPENSATIONALLY     4

    1. The Angels     5
    2. The Gentiles     5
    3. The Jews     6
    4. The Christians     12

II. SCRIPTURE DOCTRINE VIEWED DISPENSATIONALLY     14

    1. An Acceptable Standing on the Part of Man before God     14
       a. Divine Grace upon Israel     15
       b. Divine Grace upon Christians     16
    2. A Divinely Specified Manner of Life     16
    3. A Divinely Appointed Service     21
    4. A Righteous Ground Whereon God May Graciously Forgive and Cleanse the Erring     21
    5. A Clear Revelation of the Responsibility on the Human Side upon Which Divine Forgiveness and Cleansing May Be Secured     21
    6. An Effective Basis upon Which God May Be Worshiped and Petitioned in Prayer     22
    7. A Future Hope     23
       a. The Future of This Life     23
       b. Intermediate State     23
       c. Resurrection     23
       d. Eternal Life     24
       e. The Covenanted Davidic Kingdom     26

III. THE CHURCH SPECIFICALLY CONSIDERED     27

    1. Two Independent and Widely Different Purposes in the Incarnation     30
    2. Christ Revealed Two Distinct Lines of Truth     31
    3. In His Death and Resurrection the Same Two Widely Different Objectives Are Discernible     32
    4. Events Predicted for the Close of the Present Age     33
    5. Distinctions between Israel and the Church in the Coming Kingdom     33

## THE CHURCH AS AN ORGANISM

Chapter II.  General Features of the Doctrine concerning the Church                                                36

    I.   The Meaning of the Word Church                     38

    II.   The Fact of a New Divine Undertaking              40

    III.   Various Terms Employed                            42

    IV.   The First Use of the Word *Church*               43

    V.   The Church the Present Divine Purpose             44

    VI.   Four Reasons Why the Church Began at Pentecost    45

    VII.   The Church in Type and Prophecy                  46

Chapter III.  Contrasts between Israel and the Church     47

    I.   The Extent of Biblical Revelation                 47

    II.   The Divine Purpose                                47

    III.   The Seed of Abraham                              47

    IV.   Birth                                            48

    V.   Headship                                          48

    VI.   Covenants                                        49

    VII.   Nationality                                      49

    VIII.   Divine Dealing                                  49

    IX.   Dispensations                                    49

    X.   Ministry                                          50

    XI.   The Death of Christ                              50

    XII.   The Father                                       50

    XIII.   Christ                                          50

    XIV.   The Holy Spirit                                 50

    XV.   A Governing Principle                            51

    XVI.   Divine Enablement                                51

    XVII.   Two Farewell Discourses                         51

    XVIII.   The Promise of Christ's Return                 51

    XIX.   Position                                         52

    XX.   Christ's Earthly Reign                           52

    XXI.   Priesthood                                       52

XXII.    MARRIAGE                                                      52

XXIII.   JUDGMENTS                                                     52

XXIV.    POSITION IN ETERNITY                                          52

         CONCLUSION                                                    53

CHAPTER IV.   SEVEN FIGURES USED OF THE CHURCH IN HER RELA-
              TION TO CHRIST (I–V)                                     54

    I.    THE SHEPHERD AND THE SHEEP                                   56

    II.   THE VINE AND THE BRANCHES                                    59

    III.  THE CORNERSTONE AND THE STONES OF THE BUILDING              61

    IV.   THE HIGH PRIEST AND THE KINGDOM OF PRIESTS                  64

          1. The Service of Sacrifice                                 65
          2. The Service of Worship                                   66
          3. The Service of Intercession                              67

    V.    THE HEAD AND THE BODY WITH ITS MANY MEMBERS                 68

          1. The Church a Self-Developing Body                        68
          2. The Members Are Appointed to Specific Service            70
          3. The Body Is One                                          71

CHAPTER V.    SEVEN FIGURES USED OF THE CHURCH IN HER RELATION
              TO CHRIST (VI): THE LAST ADAM AND THE NEW
              CREATION                                                 79

    I.    THE RESURRECTED CHRIST                                      79

          1. The Resurrection of Christ Is Subject to Indisputable
             Proofs                                                   81
             a. The Truthfulness of Christ Himself                    81
             b. The Empty Tomb                                        81
             c. The Experience of Christ's Followers                  81
             d. The Fact of the Church                                82
             e. The Eye-Witnesses                                     82
             f. The Direct Assertion of the Bible                     83
             g. The Resurrection and the Divine Program               83
          2. The Resurrection of Christ Is Reasonable                 83
          3. Prophecy Respecting the Resurrection                     84
          4. Seven Reasons for the Resurrection                       85
             a. Because of Who Christ Is                              85
             b. To Fulfill Prophecy                                   86
             c. To Become a Bestower of Life                          86
             d. To Impart Power                                       87
             e. To Be Head to His Body, the Church                    87
             f. Resurrection and Justification                        88
             g. Christ the Pattern or First-Fruits                    89
          5. Three Standards of Power                                 90
          6. It Was an Actual Resurrection                            90

7. The Resurrection of Christ Is unto a New Order          91

II.   THE BELIEVER'S POSITION IN CHRIST          92

1. The Resurrected Christ          93
2. The New Humanity          93

III.   TWO CREATIONS REQUIRE TWO COMMEMORATION DAYS          100

1. The Biblical Testimony Regarding the Jewish Sabbath          102
   a. The Period from Adam to Moses          102
   b. The Period from Moses to Christ          104
   c. The Period Represented by the Gospels          106
   d. The Period Represented by the Acts and the Epistles          107
     (1) The Sabbath in the Book of the Acts          108
     (2) The Sabbath in the Epistles          108
   e. The Sabbath in Prophecy          111
     (1) The Cessation of the Sabbath          111
     (2) The Re-establishment of the Sabbath          111
   f. The Exact Day          112
2. The Biblical Testimony concerning the Lord's Day          113
   a. The Mosaic System Has Ceased          113
   b. A New Day Is Divinely Appointed under Grace          115
   c. A New Day Is Indicated by Important Events          116
   d. The New Day Typifies the New Creation          119
   e. The New Day Is Typical of Unmerited Grace          119
   f. The New Day Began to Be Observed with the Resurrection of Christ          120
   g. The New Day Has Been Blessed of God          122

IV.   THE FINAL TRANSFORMATION          122

1. Release from the Sin Nature          122
2. The Actual Occupation of Heavenly Citizenship          123
3. The Possession of a Transformed Body          124

CONCLUSION          126

CHAPTER VI.   SEVEN FIGURES USED OF THE CHURCH IN HER RELATION TO CHRIST (VII): THE BRIDEGROOM AND THE BRIDE          127

I.   CONTRASTED WITH ISRAEL          127

II.   A DELINEATION OF CHRIST'S KNOWLEDGE-SURPASSING LOVE          133

III.   AN ASSURANCE OF THE CONSORT'S AUTHORITY          135

IV.   A REVELATION OF THE BRIDE'S POSITION ABOVE ALL CREATED BEINGS          135

V.   A SURETY OF INFINITE GLORY          136

VI.   THE BRIDE TYPES          136
1. Eve          137

II.   THE GRACE RELATIONSHIPS                                195

1. Relationship to the Persons of the Godhead               195
2. Relation to the *Cosmos* World System                    195
   a. To Satan and His Emissaries                           195
   b. To the World System                                   196
   c. To Human Governments                                  196
   d. To the Unsaved as Individuals                         197
3. Relationship to the Body of Christ                       197
   a. A Christian's Relation to Other Christians in
      General                                               197
   b. A Christian's Relation to Those Who Are in
      Authority in the Assembly of Believers                199
   c. The Relation of Christian Husbands and Wives          199
   d. The Relation of Christian Parents and Children        200
   e. The Relation of Christian Masters and Servants        200
   f. A Christian's Obligation to an Erring Brother         200
   g. A Christian's Obligation to a Weak Brother            201

CHAPTER XI.   CONTRASTS BETWEEN LAW AND GRACE               203

I.   INDEPENDENT, SUFFICIENT, AND COMPLETE SYSTEMS OF DI-
     VINE RULE IN THE EARTH                                 205

1. The Teachings of the Law of Moses                        205
2. The Teachings of Grace                                   205
3. The Teachings of the Kingdom                             207
   a. The Similarity and Dissimilarity between the
      Teachings of the Law of Moses and the
      Teachings of Grace                                    208
   b. The Similarity and Dissimilarity between the
      Teachings of the Law of Moses and the
      Teachings of the Kingdom                              211
      (1) They Are Similar Because They Are
          Based on a Covenant of Works                      211
      (2) They Are Similar because of Elements
          Which Are Common to Both                          212
      (3) They Are Dissimilar because of Certain
          Points in Which They Differ                       213
   c. The Similarity and Dissimilarity between the
      Teachings of Grace and the Laws of the
      Kingdom                                               213
      (1) The Beatitudes                                    216
      (2) The Similitudes of the Righteous in the
          Kingdom                                           219
      (3) Christ Interprets the Law in Its Relation
          to the Kingdom                                    219
      (4) Mere Externalism Rebuked                          221
      (5) Prayer for the Kingdom, and in the
          Kingdom                                           221
      (6) The Law Governing Riches in the King-
          dom                                               222

(7) The Father's Care over the Children of
the Kingdom 222
(8) Warning Against Judgment of Others 223
(9) Warning Against False Prophets 223
(10) Three Determining Statements concerning the Kingdom 223

II. THE SEQUENCE OF THE DIVINE BLESSING AND THE HUMAN
OBLIGATION 225

III. DIFFERENT DEGREES OF DIFFICULTY AND DIFFERENT DEGREES
OF DIVINE ENABLEMENT 233

CHAPTER XII. THE LAW SYSTEMS AND JUDAISM DONE AWAY 234

I. THE ACTUAL WRITTEN INSTRUCTIONS OF BOTH THE TEACH-
INGS OF THE LAW OF MOSES AND THE KINGDOM ARE
DONE AWAY 234

1. The Passing of the Law of Moses Is the Explicit
Teaching of the New Testament Scriptures 234
2. The Error of Commingling the Law of the Kingdom
with the Teachings of Grace 243
a. The Two Systems Cannot Coexist 244
b. Not Necessary to Combine Them 245

II. THE LAW COVENANT OF WORKS IS DONE AWAY 246

III. THE LAW PRINCIPLE OF DEPENDENCE ON THE ENERGY OF
THE FLESH IS DONE AWAY 247

IV. JUDAISM IS DONE AWAY 248

CONCLUSION 249

## ESCHATOLOGY

CHAPTER XIII. INTRODUCTION TO ESCHATOLOGY 255

## GENERAL FEATURES OF ESCHATOLOGY

CHAPTER XIV. A BRIEF SURVEY OF THE HISTORY OF CHILIASM 264

I. THE PERIOD REPRESENTED BY THE OLD TESTAMENT 265

II. THE MESSIANIC KINGDOM OFFERED TO ISRAEL AT THE FIRST
ADVENT 265

III. THE KINGDOM REJECTED AND POSTPONED 266

IV. CHILIASTIC BELIEFS HELD BY THE EARLY CHURCH 267

V. THE CHILIASTIC EXPECTATION CONTINUED UNTIL THE
ROMAN APOSTASY 270

VI. CHILIASM BEGAN TO BE RESTORED IN THE REFORMATION 277

VII. CHILIASM SINCE THE REFORMATION          279
  1. The Theory of Whitby                    280
  2. Antimillennialism                       281
  3. Premillennialism                        282

CHAPTER XV. THE BIBLICAL CONCEPTION OF PROPHECY   285

  I. THE PROPHET                             285

  II. THE PROPHET'S MESSAGE                  286

  III. THE PROPHET'S POWER                   287

  IV. THE SELECTION OF PROPHETS             287

  V. THE FULFILLMENT OF PROPHECY            287

  VI. THE HISTORY OF PROPHECY               288
    1. Four Prophets Who Serve as Milestones  288
      a. Abraham                            288
      b. Moses                              289
      c. Daniel                             289
      d. Christ                             289
    2. John the Baptist                     290
    3. False Prophets                       294
    4. The Classification of Old Testament Written Prophecies   294

THE MAJOR HIGHWAYS OF PROPHECY

CHAPTER XVI. PROPHECY CONCERNING THE LORD JESUS CHRIST 296

  I. PROPHET                                299

  II. PRIEST                                300

  III. KING                                 300

  IV. THE SEED                              302

  V. THE TWO ADVENTS                        302
    1. The First Advent                     304
    2. The Second Advent                    305

CHAPTER XVII. PROPHECY CONCERNING ISRAEL'S COVENANTS   310

  I. THE FOUR MAJOR COVENANTS               313
    1. The Covenant Made with Abraham       313
    2. The Covenant Given through Moses     314
    3. The Covenant Made with David         314
    4. The New Covenant Yet to Be Made in the Messianic Kingdom   314

II.  SEVEN FEATURES                                            315

    1. A Nation Forever                                       315
    2. A Land Forever                                         317
       a. The Nation "Plucked from Off" the Land for
          Its Unfaithfulness                              317
       b. A Future Repentance of Israel                    318
       c. The Return of Messiah                            318
       d. Israel's Restoration to the Land                 318
       e. Israel's Conversion as a Nation                  320
       f. Judgment on Israel's Oppressors                  322
       g. The Nation Will Be Blessed Then                  323
    3. A King Forever                                         323
    4. A Throne Forever                                       323
    5. A Kingdom Forever                                      324
    6. A New Covenant                                         325
    7. Abiding Blessings                                      325

CHAPTER XVIII.  PROPHECY CONCERNING THE GENTILES              329

CHAPTER XIX.  PROPHECY CONCERNING SATAN, EVIL, AND THE MAN
      OF SIN                                               345

  I.  SATAN                                                   345

  II.  EVIL                                                   346

  III.  THE MAN OF SIN                                        346

CHAPTER XX.  PROPHECY CONCERNING THE COURSE AND END OF
      APOSTATE CHRISTENDOM                                 352

CHAPTER XXI.  PROPHECY CONCERNING THE GREAT TRIBULATION       360

  I.  THE DOCTRINE IN GENERAL                                 360

  II.  THE CHURCH AND THE TRIBULATION                         364

    1. The Nature of the Tribulation                         364
    2. The Nature of the Church                              365
    3. Must the Last Generation of the Church Suffer
       Especially?                                      366
    4. The Testimony of the Scriptures                       367
       a. The Imminent Return of Christ                    367
       b. The Anticipation of the Element of Time          368
       c. The Dispensational Feature                       368
       d. The Major Scripture                              369
       e. The Twenty-Four Elders                           371
       f. The Restrainer Removed                           372

CHAPTER XXII.  PROPHECY CONCERNING THE CHURCH                 374

  I.  THE LAST DAYS FOR THE CHURCH                            374

  II.  THE RESURRECTION OF THE BODIES OF THE SAINTS          375

III.   THE TRANSLATION OF LIVING SAINTS                   376

IV.   THE JUDGMENT SEAT OF CHRIST                         377

V.   THE MARRIAGE OF THE LAMB                             377

VI.   THE RETURN OF THE CHURCH WITH CHRIST               377

VII.   THE REIGN OF THE CHURCH WITH CHRIST               378

      CONCLUSION                                          378

CHAPTER XXIII. MAJOR THEMES OF OLD TESTAMENT PROPHECY     379

I.   PROPHECY RESPECTING THE GENTILES                     379
      1. The First Gentile Prediction                     379
      2. The Judgments upon Nations Adjacent to Israel     379
      3. The Times of the Gentiles                         379
      4. The Succession of Monarchies                      380
      5. The Judgment of Gentile Nations                   380
      6. Gentile Nations and the Lake of Fire              380
      7. Gentile Nations and the Kingdom                   380

II.   PROPHECY RESPECTING ISRAEL'S EARLY HISTORY          381

III.   PROPHECY RESPECTING THE NATION ISRAEL              381

IV.   PROPHECY RESPECTING THE DISPERSIONS AND THE RE-
      GATHERINGS OF ISRAEL                                 381

V.   PROPHECY RESPECTING THE ADVENT OF MESSIAH            382

VI.   PROPHECY RESPECTING THE GREAT TRIBULATION           383

VII.   PROPHECY RESPECTING THE DAY OF JEHOVAH AND THE
      MESSIANIC KINGDOM                                    383

      CONCLUSION                                           384

CHAPTER XXIV. MAJOR THEMES OF NEW TESTAMENT PROPHECY      385

I.   THE NEW AGE                                           385

II.   THE NEW DIVINE PURPOSE                              386

III.   THE NATION ISRAEL                                   387

IV.   THE GENTILES                                         388

V.   THE GREAT TRIBULATION                                388

VI.   SATAN AND THE FORCES OF EVIL                        388

VII.   THE SECOND COMING OF CHRIST                        389

VIII.   THE MESSIANIC KINGDOM                             389

IX.   THE ETERNAL STATE                                    389

      CONCLUSION                                           389

CHAPTER XXV. PREDICTED EVENTS IN THEIR ORDER    390

     I. NOAH'S PREDICTION RESPECTING HIS SONS    390

     II. ISRAEL'S BONDAGE IN EGYPT    390

     III. THE FUTURE OF JACOB'S SONS    390

     IV. ISRAEL IN THE LAND    391

     V. ISRAEL'S CAPTIVITIES    391

     VI. JUDGMENTS TO FALL UPON SURROUNDING NATIONS    391

     VII. A PARTIAL RESTORATION    391

     VIII. THE COMING AND MINISTRY OF JOHN THE BAPTIST    391

     IX. THE BIRTH OF CHRIST    392

     X. THE OFFICES OF CHRIST    392
         1. Prophet    392
         2. Priest    392
         3. King    392

     XI. THE MINISTRIES OF CHRIST    392

     XII. THE DEATH OF CHRIST    392

     XIII. THE BURIAL OF CHRIST    393

     XIV. THE RESURRECTION OF CHRIST    393

     XV. THE ASCENSION OF CHRIST    393

     XVI. THE PRESENT AGE    393

     XVII. THE DAY OF PENTECOST    393

     XVIII. THE CHURCH    394

     XIX. THE DESTRUCTION OF JERUSALEM    394

     XX. THE LAST DAYS FOR THE CHURCH    394

     XXI. THE FIRST RESURRECTION    394

     XXII. THE RAPTURE OF LIVING SAINTS    395

     XXIII. THE CHURCH IN HEAVEN    395

     XXIV. THE BELIEVER'S REWARDS    396

     XXV. THE MARRIAGE OF THE LAMB    396

     XXVI. THE GREAT TRIBULATION PER SE    396

     XXVII. THE APPEARING OF THE MAN OF SIN    397

     XXVIII. ISRAEL'S FINAL SUFFERINGS    397

     XXIX. THE DESTRUCTION OF ECCLESIASTICAL BABYLON    397

     XXX. THE BATTLE OF ARMAGEDDON    397

|  XXXI. | THE DESTRUCTION OF POLITICAL AND COMMERCIAL BABYLON | 398 |
|  XXXII. | THE DAY OF THE LORD PER SE | 398 |
|  XXXIII. | THE SECOND COMING OF CHRIST PER SE | 398 |
|  XXXIV. | SATAN BOUND AND CONFINED | 399 |
|  XXXV. | THE REGATHERING AND JUDGMENT OF SORROWING ISRAEL | 399 |
|  XXXVI. | THE JUDGMENT OF THE NATIONS | 399 |
|  XXXVII. | HUMAN LIFE IN THE EARTHLY KINGDOM | 400 |
|  XXXVIII. | THE LOOSING OF SATAN AND THE LAST REVOLT | 400 |
|  XXXIX. | THE DOOM OF SATAN | 400 |
|  XL. | THE PASSING OF THE PRESENT EARTH AND HEAVEN | 400 |
|  XLI. | THE GREAT WHITE THRONE JUDGMENT | 401 |
|  XLII. | THE DESTINY OF THE WICKED | 401 |
|  XLIII. | THE CREATION OF A NEW HEAVEN AND A NEW EARTH | 401 |
|  XLIV. | THE DESTINY OF THE SAVED | 401 |
|  XLV. | THE DAY OF GOD | 401 |
|   | CONCLUSION | 401 |

CHAPTER XXVI.  THE JUDGMENTS     402

|  I. | THE DIVINE JUDGMENTS THROUGH THE CROSS | 402 |
|  | 1. The Judgment of the Sin of the World | 402 |
|  | 2. The Judgment of the Believer's Sin Nature | 403 |
|  | 3. The Judgment of Satan through the Cross | 403 |
|  II. | THE SELF-JUDGMENT OF THE BELIEVER AND THE CHASTENING JUDGMENTS OF GOD | 403 |
|  III. | THE JUDGMENT OF THE BELIEVER'S WORKS | 404 |
|  IV. | THE JUDGMENT OF ISRAEL | 406 |
|  V. | THE JUDGMENT OF THE NATIONS | 409 |
|  VI. | THE JUDGMENT OF ANGELS | 411 |
|  VII. | THE JUDGMENT OF THE GREAT WHITE THRONE | 411 |
|  | CONCLUSION | 412 |

CHAPTER XXVII.  THE ETERNAL STATE     413

|  I. | THE INTERMEDIATE STATE | 413 |
|  | 1. Two Important Words of Location | 413 |
|  | 2. The Doctrine of Sleep | 414 |
|  | 3. An Intermediate Body | 414 |

II.   THE CREATURES OF GOD WHO ENTER THE ETERNAL STATE   415
    1. Unfallen Angels                                   415
    2. Fallen Angels                                     415
    3. Saved Gentiles                                    416
    4. Unsaved Gentiles                                  416
    5. Gentiles of the Kingdom                           416
    6. Gentiles Debarred from the Kingdom                416
    7. Jews in the Kingdom                               416
    8. Jews Excluded from the Kingdom                    417
    9. Jews Saved by Entry into the Church               417
    10. Jews Condemned for Rejecting the Gospel          418
    11. The Unsaved as a Whole                           418
    12. The Christians                                   418

III.  VARIOUS SPHERES OF EXISTENCE                       418

IV.   THEORIES RELATING TO A FUTURE STATE                420
    1. Death as Cessation of Existence                   420
    2. Transmigration of the Soul                        420
    3. Conditional Immortality                           420
    4. Universalism                                      422
    5. Restitutionism or Reconciliationism               423
    6. Rome's Purgatory                                  426
    7. Nirvana                                           426

V.    THE NEW EARTH                                      427

VI.   THE DOCTRINE OF HELL                               427

VII.  THE DOCTRINE OF HEAVEN                             433
    1. The Informed Witnesses                            434
        a. Christ                                        434
        b. Paul                                          435
        c. John                                          436
    2. The Future Estate of the Redeemed                 436
    3. Heaven the Suitable Abode of God and His People   436
    4. Some Essential Features of Heaven                 437
        a. An Abundant Life                              437
        b. Rest                                          437
        c. Knowledge                                     437
        d. Holiness                                      437
        e. Service                                       437
        f. Worship                                       437
        g. Glory                                         437
    5. The Third Heaven                                  437

    CONCLUSION                                           438

# TABLE OF CONTENTS: VOLUME V

## CHRISTOLOGY

CHAPTER I. THE PREINCARNATE CHRIST THE SON OF GOD     3

    I. THE DEITY OF CHRIST     7

       1. The Divine Names     9
         a. Designations of Eternal Relationship     9
         b. The Primary Designations of Deity     12
       2. The Evidential Attributes     17
       3. The Evidential Mighty Works     19
       4. The Triune Relationship     22

    II. CHRIST AND CREATION     23

    III. THE BEFORE-TIME COVENANT     27

    IV. THE OLD TESTAMENT MESSIAH     28

    V. THE ANGEL OF JEHOVAH     31

    VI. INDIRECT BIBLICAL IMPLICATIONS     33

    VII. DIRECT BIBLICAL ASSERTIONS     33

    CONCLUSION     38

CHAPTER II. INTRODUCTION TO THE DOCTRINE OF CHRIST INCARNATE     39

    I. THE DOCTRINE AS A WHOLE     39

    II. THE OLD TESTAMENT ANTICIPATIONS     42

       1. The Types     43
       2. The Prophecies     44

CHAPTER III. THE BIRTH AND CHILDHOOD OF CHRIST INCARNATE     47

    I. THE BIRTH     47

    II. THE CHILDHOOD     53

CHAPTER IV. THE BAPTISM OF CHRIST INCARNATE     56

    I. THE BAPTIZER     56

    II. THE NEED     59

    III. THE MODE     63

       1. The Philological Evidence     64
       2. The Exegetical Evidence     66

IV.  CHRIST'S BAPTISM AND CHRISTIAN BAPTISM                    69

V.  OTHER BAPTISMS                                            70

    1. The Baptism by the Holy Spirit                     71
    2. The Cup Baptism                                    72

CHAPTER V.  THE TEMPTATION OF CHRIST INCARNATE               74

I.  THREE FUNDAMENTAL FACTORS                              74

    1. The Meaning of πειράζω                             74
    2. God May Be Tested                                  75
    3. Christ Was Tempted                                 76

II.  CHRIST'S RELATION TO THE HOLY SPIRIT                  80

III.  CHRIST'S TESTING BY SATAN                            80

CHAPTER VI.  THE TRANSFIGURATION OF CHRIST INCARNATE        85

I.  THE IMPORTANCE                                         86

II.  THE REASON                                            87

    1. The Immediate Need                                 88
    2. The Agelong Need                                   90

III.  THE REALITY                                          90

IV.  A REPRESENTATION OF THE KINGDOM                       91

V.  THE DIVINE ATTESTATION                                 93

CHAPTER VII.  THE TEACHINGS OF CHRIST INCARNATE             95

I.  THE MAJOR DISCOURSES                                   96

    1. The Sermon on the Mount                            97
        a. Setting                                        99
        b. Distinctive Character                          102
        c. Delay in Its Application                       113
    2. The Olivet Discourse                                114
    3. The Upper Room Discourse                            140
        a. A New Relationship to God                      143
        b. Cleansing unto Unbroken Fellowship             146
        c. Abiding in Christ for Fruit Bearing            148
        d. A New Relationship to the Holy Spirit          151
        e. A New Relationship between Believers           157
        f. A New Ground of Prayer                         160
        g. The Promised Return                            164

CONCLUSION                                                166

II.  PARABLES                                              166

    1. Messianic                                          168
    2. General                                            168

III.  SPECIAL TEACHINGS                                          169

IV.  CONVERSATIONS                                               169

CHAPTER VIII.  THE MIRACLES OF CHRIST INCARNATE                  170

  CONCLUSION                                                     176

CHAPTER IX.  THE SUFFERINGS AND DEATH OF CHRIST INCARNATE        177

  I.  IN TYPES                                                   177

  II.  IN PROPHECY                                               181

      1. The Major Historical Prediction                        181
      2. The Major Doctrinal Prediction                         184
      3. Minor Predictions                                      185
      4. Christ's Predictions                                   187

  III.  IN THE SYNOPTICS                                        188

  IV.  IN JOHN'S WRITINGS                                       189

      1. The Gospel                                             189
      2. The Epistles                                           197
      3. The Revelation                                         198

  V.  IN PAUL'S WRITINGS                                        201

      1. Romans                                                 201
      2. First and Second Corinthians                          208
      3. Galatians                                              212
      4. The Prison Epistles                                    215
      5. The Thessalonian Epistles                              223
      6. The Pastoral Epistles                                  223

  VI.  IN PETER'S WRITINGS                                      224

  VII.  IN THE LETTER TO THE HEBREWS                            225

CHAPTER X.  THE RESURRECTION OF CHRIST INCARNATE                231

  I.  THE OLD TESTAMENT DOCTRINE                                234

      1. The Types                                              235
      2. The Prophecies                                         236

  II.  THE NEW TESTAMENT DOCTRINE                               238

      1. Christ's Predictions                                   239
      2. Subject to Valid Proof                                 241
      3. Actual Resurrection                                    243
      4. A New Order of Being                                   244
      5. Seven Reasons                                          245
          a. Because of Who He Is                               245
          b. To Fulfill the Davidic Covenant                   246

c. To Become the Source of Resurrection Life     247
d. To Be the Source of Resurrection Power     247
e. To Be Head over All Things to the Church     248
f. On Account of Justification     248
g. To Be the First-Fruits     249
6. The Present Standard of Divine Power     249
7. The Lord's Day a Commemoration     253
   a. The Sabbath from Adam to Moses     254
   b. The Sabbath from Moses to Christ     254
   c. The Church Age     255
   d. The Sabbath in the Coming Age     256
   e. The New Creation     256
   f. The Lord's Day     257
     (1) A New Day Prophesied and Appointed     257
     (2) Observance Indicated by Various Events     258
     (3) The Day of Circumcision     258
     (4) The Day of Grace     258
     (5) The Day Blessed of God     258
     (6) The Day Committed Only to the Individual     259
     (7) No Command to Keep the Day     259

CONCLUSION     260

CHAPTER XI. THE ASCENSION AND SESSION OF CHRIST INCARNATE     261

   I. THE ASCENSION     262

1. The Ascension on the Resurrection Morn     262
   a. Christ Entered the Heavenly Sanctuary     264
   b. Christ the First-Fruits     267
2. The Final Ascension on the Clouds of Heaven     268

   II. THE SESSION     273

1. The Exercise of Universal Authority     274
2. Head over All Things to the Church     274
3. The Bestower of Gifts     275
4. The Intercessor     276
5. The Advocate     276
6. The Builder     277
7. Christ Expecting     278

CHAPTER XII. THE SECOND ADVENT OF CHRIST INCARNATE     280

CHAPTER XIII. THE MESSIANIC KINGDOM OF CHRIST INCARNATE     315

   I. ASSURED BY JEHOVAH'S COVENANTS     317

1. The Covenant with Abraham     318
   a. An Everlasting Nation     318
   b. An Everlasting Possession of the Land     320
2. The Covenant with David     321

II. ITS VARIOUS FORMS ........................................ 333

    1. The Judges ............................................ 333

    2. The Davidic Reign and Covenant ........................ 333

    3. The Kingdom Predicted ................................. 333

        a. To Be Theocratic ................................. 334

        b. To Be Heavenly in Character ...................... 335

        c. To Be in Jerusalem and World-Wide ................ 336

        d. To Be Established by the Returning King ........... 339

        e. To Be Spiritual .................................. 339

    4. The Kingdom Offered ................................... 340

    5. The Kingdom Rejected and Postponed .................... 347

    6. The Present Form ...................................... 349

    7. The Kingdom of Heaven Realized and Manifested ......... 354

CHAPTER XIV. THE ETERNAL KINGDOM OF CHRIST INCARNATE ....... 359

    I. THE RELEASE OF SATAN ................................. 360

    II. THE REVOLT ON EARTH ................................. 360

    III. THE PASSING OF HEAVEN AND EARTH ................... 362

    IV. THE GREAT WHITE THRONE JUDGMENT .................... 363

    V. THE CREATION OF A NEW HEAVEN AND A NEW EARTH ........ 365

    VI. THE DESCENT OF THE BRIDAL CITY ..................... 366

    VII. THE SURRENDER OF THE MEDIATORIAL ASPECT ........... 368

# TABLE OF CONTENTS: VOLUME VI

## PNEUMATOLOGY

| | | |
|---|---|---|
| PREFACE | | 3 |
| CHAPTER I. THE NAME OF THE HOLY SPIRIT | | 7 |
| I. | THE THREEFOLD NAME OF DEITY | 7 |
| II. | DESCRIPTIVE TITLES | 19 |
| CHAPTER II. THE DEITY OF THE HOLY SPIRIT | | 22 |
| I. | DIVINE ATTRIBUTES | 23 |
| | 1. Eternity | 23 |
| | 2. Omnipotence | 23 |
| | 3. Omnipresence | 24 |
| | 4. Omniscience | 24 |
| | 5. Love | 24 |
| | 6. Faithfulness | 24 |
| | 7. Truthfulness | 25 |
| | 8. Holiness | 25 |
| II. | DIVINE WORKS | 26 |
| | 1. Creation | 27 |
| | 2. Striving | 28 |
| | 3. Inspiration | 28 |
| | 4. Generating Christ | 32 |
| | 5. Convincing | 33 |
| | 6. Restraining | 34 |
| | 7. Regeneration | 35 |
| | 8. Illumination | 36 |
| | 9. As a Paraclete | 38 |
| | 10. Witnessing | 39 |
| | 11. Anointing | 40 |
| | 12. Baptism | 40 |
| | 13. Sealing | 41 |
| | 14. Filling | 42 |
| | 15. Intercession | 42 |
| | 16. Sanctification | 45 |
| | 17. As an Earnest | 46 |
| | CONCLUSION | 46 |

Chapter III.  Types and Symbols of the Holy Spirit                47

    I.    OIL                                                     47

    II.   WATER                                                   50

    III.  FIRE                                                    52

    IV.  WIND                                                    52

    V.   DOVE                                                    53

    VI.  EARNEST                                                 54

    VII. SEAL                                                    54

    VIII. ABRAHAM'S SERVANT                                       55

    CONCLUSION                                              56

Chapter IV.  The Holy Spirit and Prophecy                         57

    I.   THE AUTHOR OF PROPHECY                                  57

    II.  THE SUBJECT OF PREDICTION                               60

    CONCLUSION                                              65

Chapter V.  The Holy Spirit in the Old Testament                  66

    I.   FROM ADAM TO ABRAHAM                                    66
        1. Direct References                                 66
        2. The Revealer of Truth                             69

    II.  FROM ABRAHAM TO CHRIST                                  70
        1. Indwelling                                        74
        2. Baptizing                                         74
        3. Sealing                                           74
        4. Filling                                           74

Chapter VI.  The Distinctive Character of the Present Age         80

    I.   AN INTERCALATION                                        81

    II.  A NEW DIVINE PURPOSE                                    81

    III. AN AGE OF WITNESSING                                    82

    IV.  ISRAEL DORMANT                                          83

    V.   SPECIAL CHARACTER OF EVIL                               83

    VI.  AN AGE OF GENTILE PRIVILEGE                             83

    VII. THE WORK OF THE SPIRIT WORLD-WIDE                        84

Chapter VII.  The Work of the Holy Spirit in the World            85

    I.   THE RESTRAINER OF THE *Cosmos* WORLD                    85

II.  THE ONE WHO CONVICTS THE UNSAVED                    88
    1. Of Sin                                             95
    2. Of Righteousness                                   96
    3. Of Judgment                                        97
    CONCLUSION                                            98

## THE HOLY SPIRIT IN RELATION TO THE CHRISTIAN

CHAPTER VIII.  INTRODUCTION TO THE WORK OF THE HOLY SPIRIT IN
THE BELIEVER                                                100

CHAPTER IX.  REGENERATION AND THE HOLY SPIRIT               104

  I.  THE NECESSITY                                        104

  II.  THE IMPARTATION OF LIFE                             106
    1. A Knowledge of God                              107
    2. A New Reality in Prayer                         107
    3. A New Reality in the Reading of God's Word      108
    4. A Recognition of God's Family                   108
    5. A Divine Compassion for a Lost World            108

  III.  ACQUISITION OF THE NATURE OF GOD                   109

  IV.  INDUCTION INTO THE FAMILY AND HOUSEHOLD OF GOD      110

  V.  INHERITANCE OF A SON'S PORTION                       111

  VI.  GOD'S OWN PURPOSE TO HIS ETERNAL GLORY              111

  VII.  THE BASIS IN FAITH                                 113
    CONCLUSION                                         121

CHAPTER X.  THE INDWELLING OF THE HOLY SPIRIT               122

  I.  ACCORDING TO REVELATION                              124

  II.  IN RELATION TO ANOINTING                            133

  III.  ACCORDING TO REASON                                134

  IV.  IN RELATION TO SEALING                              136

CHAPTER XI.  THE BAPTISM OF THE HOLY SPIRIT                 138

  I.  THE WORD ΒΑΠΤΙΖΩ                                     138

  II.  THE DETERMINING SCRIPTURES                          141

  III.  THE THING ACCOMPLISHED                             151
    1. Organic Union                                   152
    2. The Fourfold Prayer of Christ                   152
    3. The Only Ground for Imputed Righteousness       154

4. Due Recognition of the Union                   156
5. The Ground of Appeal for a Holy Life           157

IV.  THE DISTINCTIVENESS                          157

1. Not Regeneration                               158
2. Not Indwelling                                 158
3. Not Filling                                    159

CONCLUSION                                        159

## THE BELIEVER'S RESPONSIBILITY

CHAPTER XII.  INTRODUCTION TO THE BELIEVER'S RESPONSIBILITY    162

I.    INTELLIGENT MOTIVES                         162

II.   PRESCRIBED OBLIGATIONS                      165

III.  DEPENDENCE UPON THE SPIRIT                  167

IV.   WORD OF GOD                                 168

V.    A SPIRITUAL TRANSFORMATION                  172

VI.   THE TERMINOLOGY USED                        173

CHAPTER XIII.  POWER TO OVERCOME EVIL             177

I.    THE WORLD                                   179

II.   THE FLESH                                   183

III.  THE DEVIL                                   194

CONCLUSION                                        195

CHAPTER XIV.  POWER TO DO GOOD                    198

I.    THE FRUIT OF THE SPIRIT                     199

1. Love                                           202
   a. Inclusive of the Whole World                203
   b. Exclusive of the World System               203
   c. Inclusive of the True Church                204
   d. Without End                                 204
   e. Toward Israel                               204
   f. Sacrificial                                 204
   g. Unrequited and Pure                         205
2. Joy                                            207
3. Peace                                          208
4. Long-suffering                                 208
5. Gentleness                                     210
6. Goodness                                       211
7. Faithfulness                                   212
8. Meekness                                       213

9. Self-control                                                214

II.   THE GIFTS OF THE HOLY SPIRIT                             215

III.  THE OFFERING OF PRAISE AND THANKSGIVING                 220

IV.   THE TEACHING OF THE SPIRIT                              221

V.    THE LEADING OF THE SPIRIT                               225

VI.   THE LIFE OF FAITH                                       228

VII.  THE INTERCESSION OF THE SPIRIT                          229

      CONCLUSION                                              230

CHAPTER XV.  CONDITIONS PREREQUISITE TO FILLING              232

I.    "GRIEVE NOT THE HOLY SPIRIT OF GOD"                    234
      1. Prevention of the Christian's Sin                    235
      2. Remedy of the Christian's Sin                        236

II.   "QUENCH NOT THE SPIRIT"                                 250
      1. Resistance of the Spirit                             253
      2. The Yielded Life                                     253
      3. The Example of Christ                                256
      4. The Will of God                                      259
      5. The Sacrificial Life                                 260

III.  "WALK IN THE SPIRIT"                                    261
      1. The World                                            265
      2. The Flesh                                            265
      3. The Devil                                            266

CHAPTER XVI.  RELATED DOCTRINES                               269

I.    THE BELIEVER'S SHARE IN CHRIST'S DEATH                  275

II.   PERFECTION                                              282

III.  SANCTIFICATION                                          284

IV.   ERADICATION TEACHING                                    286

      CONCLUSION                                              288

CHAPTER XVII.  AN ANALOGY                                     290

I.    THE LOST ESTATE                                         290

II.   THE DIVINE OBJECTIVE AND IDEAL                          291

III.  THE GIFT OF GOD                                         291

IV.   THE WORK OF THE CROSS                                   292

V.    THE PLACE OF FAITH                                      293

      CONCLUSION                                              294

# TABLE OF CONTENTS: VOLUME VII

## DOCTRINAL SUMMARIZATION

| | | | |
|---|---|---|---|
| Abiding | 3 | Creeds | 101 |
| Adam | 6 | Criticism | 103 |
| Adoption | 9 | Cross | 104 |
| Advocacy | 11 | | |
| Angels | 13 | Darkness | 106 |
| Anthropology | 15 | Days | 108 |
| Antichrist | 16 | Death | 112 |
| Apostasy | 17 | Demonology | 115 |
| Ascension | 19 | Depravity | 118 |
| Assurance | 21 | Disciples | 120 |
| Atonement | 25 | Dispensations | 121 |
| Authority | 27 | Dispersions of Israel | 123 |
| | | | |
| Babylon | 29 | Ecclesiology | 127 |
| Baptism, Real | 32 | Elders | 130 |
| Baptism, Ritual | 34 | Election | 132 |
| Bibliology | 43 | Eschatology | 138 |
| Blasphemy | 46 | Eternity | 140 |
| Blindness | 49 | Evangelism | 142 |
| Blood | 52 | Evolution | 146 |
| Body | 55 | | |
| Bread | 58 | Faith | 146 |
| Bride | 60 | Fall | 149 |
| Buried | 63 | Fatherhood of God | 151 |
| | | First-Fruits | 153 |
| Calling | 65 | Flesh | 155 |
| Carnality | 68 | Foreknowledge | 158 |
| Chastisement | 70 | Foreordination | 160 |
| Christian | 73 | Forgiveness | 161 |
| Christianity | 75 | | |
| Christology | 78 | Genealogy | 166 |
| Cleansing | 83 | Gentiles | 168 |
| Commandments | 85 | Gentile Times | 170 |
| Confession | 88 | Glory | 172 |
| Conscience | 91 | God | 173 |
| Conversion | 93 | Gospel | 175 |
| Conviction | 94 | Government | 177 |
| Covenants | 96 | Grace | 178 |
| Creation | 99 | Guilt | 179 |

| | | | | |
|---|---|---|---|---|
| Hades | 180 | Messiah | 236 |
| Headship | 182 | Millennium | 237 |
| Healing | 183 | Ministry | 238 |
| Heart | 185 | Miracle | 239 |
| Heaven | 186 | Mystery | 239 |
| Holiness | 188 | | |
| Hope | 189 | Name | 240 |
| Horn | 189 | Natural Man | 241 |
| Humility | 190 | Numbers | 241 |
| | | | |
| Immortality | 190 | Obedience | 242 |
| Imputation | 191 | Omnipotence | 243 |
| Incarnation | 194 | Omnipresence | 243 |
| Infant Salvation | 196 | Omniscience | 244 |
| Infinity | 199 | Only-Begotten | 245 |
| Inheritance | 200 | Ordain | 245 |
| Innocence | 200 | Ordinance | 246 |
| Inspiration | 200 | | |
| Intercession | 201 | Paraclete | 247 |
| Intermediate State | 202 | Paradise | 247 |
| Interpretation | 203 | Parousia | 248 |
| Israel | 205 | Pauline Theology | 248 |
| | | Peace | 249 |
| Jehovah | 207 | Perfection | 250 |
| Jerusalem | 208 | Power | 251 |
| Jesus | 210 | Praise | 252 |
| Judaism | 211 | Prayer | 252 |
| Judgment | 213 | Preaching | 254 |
| Just, The | 217 | Predestination | 255 |
| Justice | 218 | Priesthood | 256 |
| Justification | 218 | Prophecy | 257 |
| | | Propitiation | 258 |
| King | 223 | Providence | 260 |
| Kingdom | 223 | Punishment | 260 |
| | | | |
| Law | 225 | Reconciliation | 262 |
| Life | 226 | Redemption | 263 |
| Logos | 227 | Regeneration | 264 |
| Lord's Day | 228 | Repentance | 265 |
| Lord's Supper | 229 | Resurrection | 266 |
| Love | 230 | Revelation | 268 |
| | | Rewards | 269 |
| Man of Sin | 232 | Righteousness | 270 |
| Marriage | 233 | | |
| Mediation | 234 | Sabbath | 270 |
| Mercy | 235 | Sacrifice | 271 |
| Mercy Seat | 236 | | |

# AUTHOR INDEX

# AUTHOR INDEX

## A

Abbott, E. A.:
IV, 370—cited by Thiessen.

Alexander, A. B. D., "Logos," International Standard Bible Encyclopaedia; Howard-Severance Co., Chicago, 1915:
III, 13; V, 10.

Alexander, W. Lindsay, A System of Biblical Theology; T. & T. Clark, Edinburgh, 1888:
I, 6, 261, 267 f., 272, 284—citation of Calvin; I, 284 f.—citation of Swift; I, 285—citation of Pye Smith; I, 285—citation of Nicene Creed; I, 285—citation of Athanasian Creed; I, 285 f., 323—citation of Socinus; II, 215 f., 216—citation of Milton; II, 221, 221 f.—citations of Aristotle, Plutarch, Kant, Hahn; III, 13 ff., 68–72, 195, 198—citation of Owen; III, 199—citation of Owen; III, 212.

Alford, Henry, New Testament for English Readers; Lee and Shepard, Boston, 1872:
I, xii, 254 f.; II, 3, 69, 70, 72—citation of Chrysostom; II, 82 f.; III, 114 f.—citation of Delitzsch; III, 248, 325—citation of Chrysostom; III, 325 f.—citation of De Wette; IV, 362—cited by Thiessen; IV, 369 f.—cited by Thiessen; V, 10, 11, 27, 34 f., 60, 127, 196, 200 f., 210, 221 f., 271 f.; VI, 43, 143, 230.

Anderson, Sir Robert, The Coming Prince, 2nd ed.; Pickering & Inglis, London, 1909:
IV, 128, 130, 289, 338—cited by Thiessen.

Angus-Green, Cyclopedic Handbook of the Bible:
VII, 204 (twice), 205 (twice)—cited by Rollin T. Chafer.

Anselm, Cur Deus Homo:
III, 137—cited by Dale.

Aristotle:
I, 291—cited by Cooke; II, 221 f.—cited by Alexander; II, 294 f.

Atwood, John M., "Universalist Church," Encyclopædia Britannica, 14th ed., New York:
IV, 422.

Auberlen, C. A.:
II, 185—cited by Laidlaw; IV, 278—cited by Peters; V, 316—cited by Peters.

Augustine:
I, 6—cited by Shedd; I, 229—cited by Shedd; I, 282—cited by Harris; I, 284 —cited by Scofield; II, 29—cited by Gerhart; II, 31 f.—cited by Gerhart; II, 212 f.; III, 57—cited by Shedd.


## B

Barclay, Robert, Apology:
I, 13.

Bardesanes:
IV, 121.

Barnabas:
IV, 121.

Barnes, Albert:
IV, 262—cited by Peters; V, 374—cited by Peters.

Baur:
III, 145 f.—cited by Miley.

Bavinck, Herman, "The Fall," International Standard Bible Encyclopaedia; Howard-Severance Co., Chicago, 1915:
VII, 149 f.

Baxter, Richard:
I, 289—cited by Watson.

Beecher, Henry Ward:
V, 287—cited by Peters.

Bengel:
IV, 278—cited by Brookes, in turn by Peters.

Besser:
II, 308—cited by Riddle.

Binney, Thomas:
III, 365 f.

Boettner, Loraine, The Inspiration of the Scriptures:
VI, 58—cited by Walvoord.

Bowne:
I, 150 f.—cited by Miley; I, 201 f.—cited by Miley.

Bradbury, John W.:
VI, 147 f.

Brewster, D.:
I, 289.

Briggs, C. A.:
IV, 283—cited by Peters.

Brookes, James H.:
III, 305—The Truth (Vol. XIII); IV, 278—citation of Bengel, in turn cited by Peters.

Brown, Jamieson & Fausset, The Critical and Explanatory Commentary; Zondervan Publishing House, Grand Rapids, 1934:
II, 301 f., 308 ff.; VI, 67.

Bruce, A. B., The Humiliation of Christ:
I, 379—cited by Feinberg; I, 380—cited by Feinberg.

Bruch, J. F.:
I, 214—cited by Van Oosterzee.

Bull:
II, 19—cited by Gaebelein.

Bullinger, E. W., Companion Bible; Oxford University Press, London, 1910:
VI, 28.

——, A Critical Lexicon and Concordance to the English and Greek New Testament, 6th rev. ed.; Longmans, Green & Co., London, 1914:
VII, 180, 180 f., 181 f.

Bush:
V, 375—cited by Peters.

Bushnell, Horace:
I, 309 f.—cited by Harris; VII, 198—cited by Hamilton.

Butler:
I, 76 f.—cited by Manly; II, 212—cited by Watson.

Buttmann-Thayer:
IV, 370—cited by Thiessen.

Buxtorf:
I, 265—cited by Watson; I, 268—cited by Watson.

## C

Calvin, John:
I, 131—cited by Strong; I, 284—cited by Alexander; II, 283—cited by Shedd; III, 69—cited by Alexander; IV, 278—cited by Peters; IV, 279—cited by Haldeman; VI, 115—cited by Walvoord.

Carlyle, Thomas:
I, 176—cited by Strong; II, 280—cited by Shedd.

Carson, Alexander:
I, 83—cited by Manly.

Carver, William Owen, "Atonement," International Standard Bible Encyclopaedia; Howard-Severance Co., Chicago, 1915:
VII, 27.

Castenove:
I, 32—cited by Rogers.

Cellerier, J. E.:
VII, 204 (twice), 205—cited by Rollin T. Chafer.

Chafer, Rollin Thomas, The Science of Biblical Hermeneutics; Bibliotheca Sacra, Dallas, 1938:
V, 349 f.; VII, 203 ff.

Chalmers, Thomas, Natural Theology:
I, 182.

——, Institutes of Theology, Thomas Constable & Co., Edinburgh, 1852:
II, 221.

Channing, William Ellery:
I, 274; III, 62 f.—cited by Stock.

Charles:
IV, 362—cited by Thiessen.

Charnocke:
I, 193—cited by Shedd.

Chrysostom:
II, 72—cited by Alford; III, 325—cited by Alford.

Cicero:
I, 154—cited by Cooke; I, 292—cited by Cooke.

Clarke, Adam:
I, 195—cited by Cooke.

Clarke, Samuel:
I, 134, 161—cited by Dick; I, 220 f.—cited by Dick.

Clarke, William Newton, An Outline of Christian Theology; Charles Scribner's Sons, New York, 1898:
V, 283 f., 284 ff.

Clement of Alexandria:
IV, 121.

Cocceius, Johannes:
V, 286, 288; VII, 96.

Cook, Joseph:
I, 284—cited by Strong.

Cooke, R. J.:
VII, 198—cited by Hamilton.

Cooke, William, Christian Theology; Partridge and Oakey, London, 1848:
II, 4 f., 12 f., 15, 16, 21 f., 37—citation of Plutarch; II, 74 f., 97—citation of Plutarch; V, 14 ff., 20; VI, 12–16, 26.

——, The Deity, 2nd ed.; Hamilton, Adams & Co., London, 1892:
I, 137 f., 146—citation of Wollaston; I, 154—citation of Cicero; I, 154 f., 174 —citation of "Veids"; I, 174—citation of Lucan; I, 174—citation of Seneca; I, 174—citation of Mason Good; I, 175, 175 f., 180 f.—citation of King; I, 195 —citation of Adam Clarke; I, 196—citation of Edwards; I, 197—citation of Mohammedan proverb; I, 198—citation of Seneca; I, 198, 290—citation of Feltham; I, 291—citation of Aristotle; I, 292—citation of Cicero.

Coquerel, M.:
I, 273—cited by Rice.

Cowper, William:
VI, 126.

Crawford, T. J., The Doctrine of Holy Scripture Respecting the Atonement; William Blackwood & Sons, Edinburgh and London, 1871:
III, 63 ff.

Cremer, A. H., Biblico-Theological Lexicon of N. T. Greek, 2nd ed.; English translation by W. Urwick; T. & T. Clark, Edinburgh, 1872:
I, 79.

Crisp:
III, 70 f.—cited by Alexander from Williams.

Cudworth:
I, 145 f.—cited by Watson.

Cumming, J. Elder:
VI, 19 f.—cited by Walvoord.

Cunningham, William, Historical Theology, 3rd ed.; T. & T. Clark, Edinburgh, 1870:
I, 387—citation of Westminster Confession; I, 387 f.; III, 269, 270, 271, 277 f., 284 f.

Cyprian, Bishop of Carthage:
IV, 120.

## D

Dabney, R. L.:
IV, 256.

Dale, James W., Christic and Patristic Baptism; William Rutter & Co., Philadelphia, 1874:
III, 41 f., 381 ff., 383 f.; V, 71 f.

——, Johannic Baptism; Presbyterian Board of Publication and Sabbath School Work, Philadelphia, 1871:
V, 59—citation of Gregory Thaumaturgus; V, 68—citation of R. Wilson; V, 69.

——, Classic Baptism; William Rutter & Co., Philadelphia, 1867:
VI, 139.

——:
VI, 149 f.—cited by Unger; VII, 32, 33.

Dale, R. W., The Atonement; Hodder & Stoughton, London, 1875:
III, 44—citation of Turretin; III, 132 f., 136—citation of Epistle to Diognetus; III, 136 f.—citation of Gregory Nazianzen; III, 137—citation of Anselm; III, 138—citation of Luther; III, 152 f.

Darby, J. N., Synopsis of the Books of the Bible; Loizeaux Bros., New York:
III, 123.

Davidson, A. B., Theology of the Old Testament; T. & T. Clark, Edinburgh, 1904:
I, 260, 406—cited by Warfield; V, 45—cited by Walvoord.

Dawson:
II, 140 f.—cited by Miley.

Delitzsch, Franz:
I, 265—cited by Oehler; II, 136—cited by Laidlaw; III, 114 f.—cited by Alford.

Denney, James:

I, 402 f.—cited by Warfield; II, 288 f.—cited by Thomas; V, 243—cited by Harrison.

———, The Atonement and the Modern Mind; A. C. Armstrong & Son, New York, 1903:

III, 43 f.

De Wette:

III, 325 f.—cited by Alford.

Dibelius, Martin, The Sermon on the Mount; Charles Scribner's Sons, New York, 1940:

V, 102, 113.

Dick, John, Lectures on Theology; Applegate & Co., Cincinnati, 1864:

I, 16, 16 f., 49—citations of Plato and Socrates; I, 161, 219, 220, 220 f.—citation of Samuel Clarke; I, 221 f., 242 f., 252, 283—cited by Wardlaw; I, 371; III, 300 f.

Dietrich:

I, 265—cited by Oehler.

Dillmann:

VII, 159—cited by Hodge.

Dods, Marcus:

III, 159 f.—cited by Warfield.

Doederlein, John C.:

I, 288—cited by Harris.

Dorner, I. A., History of Protestant Theology; T. & T. Clark, Edinburgh, 1871:

I, 377; II, 9; IV, 256.

Drummond, Henry, Addresses; Donohue, Henneberg & Co., Chicago:

VII, 230.

Dunelm, Handley:

See H. C. G. Moule.

Dwight, Timothy, Theology:

I, 144—cited by Watson; II, 221, 293.


E

Edwards, Jonathan:

I, 196—cited by Cooke; II, 164—cited by Watson; II, 170—cited by Laidlaw; III, 71 f.—cited by Alexander.

English, E. Schuyler, Studies in the Gospel according to Matthew; Fleming H. Revell Co., New York, 1935:
V, 106.

Eusebius:
IV, 120.

Everett, Theism and the Christian Faith:
I, 132.


**F**

Fairbairn, A. M., Christ in Modern Theology; Hodder & Stoughton, London, 1902:
II, 267.

Fairbairn, Patrick, The Typology of Scripture; Funk & Wagnalls, New York, 1900:
I, xxix; III, 116.

Fairchild, Edmund B.:
VI, 149—cited by Unger.

Fausset, Jamieson & Brown, The Critical and Explanatory Commentary; Zondervan Publishing House, Grand Rapids, 1934:
II, 301 f., 308 ff.; VI, 67.

Feinberg, Charles Lee, Bibliotheca Sacra; Dallas:
I, 379 ff., 394 f., 396.

Feltham, Owen:
I, 290—cited by Cooke.

Fenelon, Archbishop Francis S.:
VII, 190—cited by Marsh.

Fichte, I. H.:
I, 137—cited by Harris.

Fisher, George Park, The Grounds of Theistic and Christian Belief, rev. ed.; Charles Scribner's Sons, New York, 1902:
I, 165 f.

Flammarion, Camille:
II, 6—cited by Gaebelein.

Foster:
III, 158—cited by Warfield.

Foster, John:
I, 164—cited by Miley.

Foster, R. S.:
I, 159.

Fremantle:
III, 161—cited by Warfield.


# G

Gaebelein, Arno C., Angels of God; Our Hope, New York, 1924:
II, 3, 6—citation of Flammarion; II, 7, 14, 19—citation of Bull.

——, Annotated Bible; Our Hope, New York:
IV, 57 f.

——, Studies in Zechariah; Francis E. Fitch, New York:
V, 186 f.

Gaussen, S. R. L., Theopneusty; John S. Taylor & Co., New York, 1842:
VI, 30 f.

Gerhart, E. V., Institutes of the Christian Religion; Vol. I published by A. C. Armstrong & Son, New York, 1891; Vol. II published by Funk & Wagnalls, New York, 1891:
II, 7—citation of Hooker; II, 9, 10—citation of Martensen; II, 25—citation of von Gerlach; II, 25 f., 29—citation of Augustine; II, 29 f.—citation of Hooker; II, 30—citation of Hooker; II, 31, 31 f.—citation of Augustine; II, 33—citation of Meyer; II, 34 f., 83—citation of Pope & Moulton; II, 112.

Gieseler:
I, 283—cited by Harris.

Godet:
I, 205—cited by Vincent; IV, 89—cited by Thomas; VII, 159—cited by Hodge.

Goff, John, How Was Jesus Baptized and Why?:
V, 64.

Good, Mason:
I, 174—cited by Cooke.

Gordon, A. J., The Ministry of the Spirit; American Baptist Publication Society, Philadelphia, 1894:
VI. 10 ff.

Gore, Charles, The Incarnation of the Son of God; Charles Scribner's Sons, New York, 1891:
I, 349 f.

Govett, R., Exposition of the Gospel of St. John; Bemrose & Sons, London:
V, 10 f., 35 f., 196.

Grant, F. W., The Numerical Bible; Loizeaux Bros., New York:
II, 307; III, 185; IV, 58 f.; V, 264 ff., 268.

Graves, Richard:
I, 280—cited by Watson.

Gray, James M., Christian Workers Commentary; Fleming H. Revell Co., New York, 1915:
VI, 67.

Gregory Nazianzen:
III, 136 f.—cited by Dale.

Green, W. H.:
II, 139—cited by Miley; II, 141—cited by Hodge.

Greene, Samuel, Present Day Tracts—Christology, "The Divinity of Jesus Christ":
I, 345.

Guille, George E., Isaac and Rebekah; Bible Institute Colportage Assn., Chicago, 1914:
VI, 55.

H

Hagenbach:
IV, 261—cited by Peters.

Hahn, G. L.:
II, 222—cited by Alexander.

Haldeman, I. M., History of Doctrine of Our Lord's Return; I. M. Haldeman, First Baptist Church, New York:
IV, 275 ff., 278—citation of Luther; IV, 279—citation of Calvin, Knox, Latimer.

———:
IV, 278—cited by Unger.

Hall, Robert, sermon on "The Spirituality of the Divine Nature":
I, 182.

Hamilton:
I, 138.

Hamilton, Alan Herbert, Bibliotheca Sacra; Dallas:
VII, 197 f., 198 f.

Hampden:
I, 22 f.—cited by Rogers.

Harnack, Adolf:
V, 53—cited by Warfield.

Harris, Samuel, God the Creator and Lord of All; T. & T. Clark, Edinburgh, Vol. I, 1896, Vol. II, 1897:
I, 184—citation of Voltaire; I, 216 f., 282—citation of Augustine; I, 282 f.—citation of Tertullian; I, 283—citation of Athanasian Creed; I, 283—citation of Gieseler; I, 283—citation of Westminster Larger Catechism; I, 283, 286—citation of Neander; I, 286 f.—citation of Orr; I, 288—citation of South; I, 288—citation of Doederlein; I, 309 f.—citation of Bushnell; I, 376 f.

——, The Philosophical Basis of Theism. rev. ed.; Charles Scribner's Sons, New York, 1883:
I, 133 f., 137—citation of Fichte.

——, The Self-Revelation of God; Charles Scribner's Sons, New York, 1892:
I, 133, 159 f.

Harrison, Everett F., Christian Doctrine of Resurrection, 1938, unpublished:
V, 241, 241 f.

Harrison, Norman B., His Love; The Harrison Service, Minneapolis:
VI, 203.

Hawes, E. E.:
VI, 150—cited by Unger.

Hawthorne, R. R., Bibliotheca Sacra; Dallas:
VI, 70.

Heard, J. B.:
II, 147—cited by Laidlaw.

Henry, Matthew, Commentary; Fleming H. Revell Co., New York:
II, 202; VI, 27, 68.

Hesiod:
II, 5—cited by Cooke.

Hibbard, F. G.:
VII, 198—cited by Hamilton.

Hodge, A. A., Outlines of Theology; A. C. Armstrong & Son, New York, 1878:
I, 156, 164, 172, 213 f., 255, 316—citation of Nicene Creed; II, 141—citation of Green; III, 211 f.; V, 27 f.

Hodge, Charles A., Systematic Theology; Charles Scribner & Co., New York, 1872:
I, 6, 67, 143 f., 160, 284; II, 175 ff.; III, 178, 180 f., 330; IV, 255; V, 85.

——, Commentary on the Epistle to the Romans, 1854:
II, 302.

——, A Commentary on the Epistle to the Ephesians; Robert Carter and Bros., New York, 1856:
V, 218 f.

——:
II, 312—cited by Schaff; II, 309—cited by Jamieson, Fausset & Brown; VI, 115—cited by Walvoord.

Hodge, Caspar Wistar, "Foreknow, Foreknowledge," International Standard Bible Encyclopaedia; Howard-Severance Co., Chicago, 1915:
VII, 158 f., 159 f.

Hogg, C. F., and W. E. Vine, Epistle to the Galatians; Pickering & Inglis, London, 1922:
V, 213, 213 f.

Hooker, Richard:
II, 7—cited by Gerhart; II, 29 f.—cited by Gerhart; II, 30—cited by Gerhart; IV, 259—cited by Peters.

Horsley, Samuel:
II, 204—cited by Watson.

Hort, and Westcott:
I, 87—cited by Manly.

Howe, John:
I, 147—cited by Watson; I, 147 ff.—cited by Watson; I, 210—cited by Watson; I, 236 f.—cited by Shedd; II, 162—cited by Watson.

Hutchinson, John, Lectures on St. Paul's Epistle to the Philippians; T. & T. Clark, Edinburgh, 1887:
V, 36 ff.

Huxley, Julian S., "Evolution," Encyclopædia Britannica, 14th ed., New York:
I, 167, 168.

——:
I, 169—cited by Hodge.

# I

Ignatius, Bishop of Antioch:
IV, 121.

Irenaeus, Bishop of Lyons:
IV, 121, 259 f.—cited by Peters from Neander.

Ironside, H. A., Lectures on Daniel; Loizeaux Bros., New York, 1920:
IV, 335 f., 348—cited by Thiessen; V, 294 f.

——, Lectures on Revelation; Loizeaux Bros., New York, 1919:
IV, 55 f.

——, Notes on the Minor Prophets; Loizeaux Bros., New York:
V, 187.

——, Notes on the Proverbs; Loizeaux Bros., New York, 1907:
V, 270 f.

# J

Jamieson, Fausset & Brown, The Critical and Explanatory Commentary; Zondervan Publishing House, Grand Rapids, 1934:
II, 301 f., 308 ff.; VI, 67.

Janet, Paul:
I, 152—cited by Miley; I, 152 f.—cited by Miley; I, 157—cited by Miley.

Jennings, F. C., Satan; A. C. Gaebelein, New York:
II, 44, 55 f., 97 f.

Justin Martyr:
IV, 121.

# K

Kant, Immanuel:
II, 222—cited by Alexander; II, 295; VII, 91.

Keith, Sir Arthur, "Evolution of Man," Encyclopædia Britannica, 14th ed., New York:
II, 132 ff.

Kelly, William, Lectures Introductory to the Study of the Minor Prophets, 5th ed.; A. S. Rouse, London, 1906:
VI, 63.

Kelly, William, Lectures on the New Testament Doctrine of the Holy Spirit; A. S. Rouse, London, 1867:
VI, 39.

Kennett:
IV, 82 f.—cited by Thomas.

Keyser, Leander, A System of Natural Theism, 2nd ed., rev., 1927, The Lutheran Literary Board, Burlington, Iowa.
I, 166.

King, William:
I, 180 f.—cited by Cooke; II, 208 f.—cited by Watson.

Knox, John:
IV, 279—cited by Haldeman.

Kuyper, A.:
VI, 69—cited by Walvoord.

**L**

Laidlaw, R. A., Bible Doctrine of Man; T. & T. Clark, Edinburgh, 1879:
II, 127—citation of Row; II, 136—citation of MacDonald; II, 136—citation of Delitzsch; II, 137, 147, 147 f., 155 f., 166—citation of Müller; II, 169 f., 170—citation of Oehler; II, 170—citation of Edwards; II, 170 ff., 185—citation of Auberlen; II, 185 ff., 191 f.

Lange:
I, 256—cited by Van Oosterzee; I, 374—cited by Peters.

Larkin, Clarence, The Spirit World; Clarence Larkin Estate, Philadelphia, 1921:
II, 114 f., 115 ff., 117.

Latimer:
IV, 279—cited by Haldeman.

Lawson:
I, 135 footnote—cited by Watson.

Leland:
I, 143—cited by Watson.

Lepsius:
I, 395.

Lewis, Charles Lee:
II, 127 f.—citation of M. F. Maury.

Lightfoot, J. B., Epistle to the Philippians; Macmillan and Co., New York, 1890:
V, 38.

——, Epistle to the Colossians; Macmillan and Co., New York, 1886:
V, 10, 24.

Lindsay, James, "Biblical Theology," International Standard Bible Encyclopaedia; Howard-Severance Co., Chicago, 1915:
I, 4.

Locke:
I, 147—cited by Watson.

Lockhart, Clinton:
VII, 204—cited by Rollin T. Chafer.

Lucan:
I, 174—cited by Cooke.

Luering, H. L. E., "Blood and Water," International Standard Bible Encyclopaedia; Howard-Severance Co., Chicago, 1915:
VII, 54 f.

Luther, Martin, Commentary on Galatians; Robert Carter & Bros., New York, 1860:
V, 214 f.

——:
III, 138—cited by Dale; IV, 260—cited by Peters; IV, 278—cited by Peters from Walch and by Haldeman.


**M**

Mabie, Henry C., The Meaning and Message of the Cross, 2nd ed.; Fleming H. Revell Co., New York, 1906:
II, 271; III, 44—citation of Dale; III, 45, 46 f., 59 f.

MacDonald:
II, 136—cited by Laidlaw.

Mackintosh, C. H., Notes on Genesis, 4th Amer. ed.; Loizeaux Bros., New York, 1879:
VI, 53 f., 67.

——, Notes on Exodus; Loizeaux Bros., New York:
III, 119 f., 120 f.

Mackintosh, C. H., Notes on Leviticus; Loizeaux Bros., New York, 1879:
III, 39 f.; V, 267 f.; VI, 48.

Maclaren, Alexander:
III, 379—cited by Pierson.

Manly, Basil, Bible Doctrine of Inspiration; A. C. Armstrong & Son, New York, 1888:
I, 72—citation of Olshausen; I, 75, 75—citation of Schaff; I, 76, 76 f.—citation of Butler; I, 83—citation of Carson; I, 87—citation of Westcott & Hort; I, 87 f.—citation of Schaff.

Marais, J. I., "Psychology," International Standard Bible Encyclopaedia; Howard-Severance Co., Chicago, 1915:
II, 126 f., 185.

——, "Soul," International Standard Bible Encyclopaedia; Howard-Severance Co., Chicago, 1915:
II, 182 ff.

——, "Spirit," International Standard Bible Encyclopaedia; Howard-Severance Co., Chicago, 1915:
II, 184 f.

Marett, Ralph Ranulph, "Anthropology," Encyclopædia Britannica, 14th ed.; New York:
II, 126.

Marsh, F. E., Emblems of the Holy Spirit, late ed.; Pickering & Inglis, London, 1923:
VI, 52; VII, 190—citation of Fenelon.

Martensen, H. L., Christian Dogmatics, translated by Wm. Urwick; T. & T. Clark, Edinburgh, 1866:
V, 76 f.

——:
II, 9 f.—cited by Gerhart; II, 10—cited by Gerhart.

Masterman, E. W. G., "Jerusalem," International Standard Bible Encyclopaedia; Howard-Severance Co., Chicago, 1915:
VII, 208.

Mather, Cotton:
IV, 280—cited by Peters.

Matheson, George:
II, 283 f.—cited by Thomas.

Matthews, Burt L.:
III, 294.

Mauro, Philip, God's Gift and Our Response; Pickering & Inglis, Glasgow:
VI, 186.

Maury, Matthew Fontaine:
II, 127 f.—cited by Lewis.

McConnell, Francis J., "Sin," International Standard Bible Encyclopaedia;
Howard-Severance Co., Chicago, 1915:
II, 241 f.

McFarland, J. T.:
VII, 198—cited by Hamilton.

McTaggart, J. M. E., Some Dogmas on Religion:
II, 92.

Medley, Samuel:
V, 3.

Melanchthon:
II, 288—cited by Müller; IV, 262 f.—cited by Peters.

Meyer, H. A. W., Commentary on the New Testament (at John 11:49–52);
T. & T. Clark, Edinburgh, 1876:
V, 195.

——:
II, 33—cited by Gerhart; II, 347—cited by Moule; VII, 159—cited by Hodge.

Middleton:
III, 382 f.—cited by Dale.

Miley, John, Systematic Theology (II Volumes); The Methodist Book Concern, New York, 1892, 1894:
I, 150 f.—citation of Bowne; I, 152—citation of Janet; I, 152, 152 f.—citation of Janet; I, 157—citation of Janet; I, 164—citation of John Foster; I, 170, 186, 201—citation of Miller; I, 201 f.—citation of Bowne; I, 218, 316, 387—citation of Schaff; I, 388 f.; II, 138 f., 139 ff.—citation of Dawson; III, 146—citation of Baur; III, 146–52.

Miller, Hugh:
I, 201—cited by Miley.

Milton, John:
II, 8—cited by Strong; II, 216—cited by Alexander.

Mivart, George, Lessons from Nature:
II, 147 f.

Moffat:
IV, 362—cited by Thiessen; IV, 370—cited by Thiessen.

Moorehead:
IV, 370—cited by Thiessen.

Morgan, G. Campbell, The Spirit of God; Fleming H. Revell Co., New York, 1890:
VI, 150.

Moule, H. C. G., Cambridge Bible, Romans; Cambridge University Press, 1908:
II, 274, 304 f., 346, 347; IV, 88 f.

——, Cambridge Bible, Colossians and Philemon; Cambridge University Press, 1906:
IV, 95 f.

——, Outlines of Christian Doctrine, 2nd rev. ed.:
VI, 294.

——, "Faith," International Standard Bible Encyclopaedia; Howard-Severance Co., Chicago, 1915:
VII, 147 f.

——:
I, 227; VII, 189.

Moulton and Pope:
II, 83—cited by Gerhart.

Müller, Julius, The Christian Doctrine of Sin; T. & T. Clark, Edinburgh, 1868:
II, 225, 237–41, 258 f., 266, 284, 288—citation of Melanchthon; II, 290 f.

——:
II, 166—cited by Laidlaw; II, 363—cited by Shedd; IV, 279—cited by Peters.

Müller, Max:
IV, 420—cited by New Standard Dictionary.

**N**

Nares, Edward:
I, 322 f.—cited by Watson.

Neander:
I, 286—cited by Harris; IV, 259 f.—cited by Peters; V, 85—cited by Peters; V, 374.

Newell, W. R., Romans Verse by Verse; Grace Publications, Inc., Chicago, 1938:
VI, 44 f.

Newton, Isaac:
I, 135 footnote—cited by Watson; I, 183 f.—cited by Watson.

Nitzsch:
IV, 425—cited by Van Oosterzee.

Nuelson, John L., "Regeneration," International Standard Bible Encyclopaedia; Howard-Severance Co., Chicago, 1915:
VI, 36.

# O

Oehler, Gustav Friedrich, Old Testament Theology; Funk & Wagnalls Co., New York, 1883:
I, 263, 405; II, 167, 170—cited by Laidlaw.

Olsen, Erling C., Meditations in the Psalms (II Volumes); Fleming H. Revell Co., New York, 1939:
V, 237, 269.

——, Walks with Our Lord through John's Gospel; Fleming H. Revell Co., New York, 1939:
V, 192 f.

Olshausen:
I, 71 f.—cited by Manly.

Orr, James, "Criticism of the Bible," International Standard Bible Encyclopaedia; Howard-Severance Co., Chicago, 1915:
VII, 103 f.

——:
I, 286 f.—cited by Harris.

Ottman, Ford C., Imperialism and Christ; Charles C. Cook, New York, 1912:
V, 328, 329–32.

——, Unfolding of the Ages; Baker & Taylor Co., New York, 1905:
IV, 354–57, 371; V, 310–314.

Ovid:
II, 194—cited by Vincent.

Owen, John:
I, 400—cited by Watson; III, 69 ff.—cited by Alexander; III, 198—cited by Alexander; III, 199—cited by Alexander.

## P

Paley, William:
I, 146 f.—cited by Watson; I, 153 f.—cited by Watson.

Parker, Theodore:
I, 36—cited by Rogers.

Pearson, John:
I, 400 f.—cited by Watson.

Peter, Bishop of Alexandria:
IV, 120.

Peters, George N. H., The Theocratic Kingdom (III Volumes); Funk & Wagnalls Co., New York, 1884:
IV, 258, 259—citation of Rothe; IV, 259 f., 261—citation of Hagenbach; IV, 262 f., 270 f.—citation of Justin Martyr; IV, 271-74, 275—citation of Whitby; IV, 278—citations of Brookes and Auberlen, Luther, Calvin; IV, 279—citation of Augsburg Confession from Müller; IV, 280—citation of Cotton Mather; IV, 283—citation of Briggs; IV, 283 f., 324 f.; V, 85—citation of Neander; V, 91 ff., 281, 287—citation of Beecher; V, 354 f., 374 ff.

Pierson, Arthur T.:
III, 379 f.

Pinches, T. G., International Standard Bible Encyclopaedia; Howard-Severance Co., Chicago, 1915:
VII, 29.

Plato:
I, 49—cited by Dick; I, 150—cited by Bowne; I, 162; II, 194—cited by Vincent.

Plummer:
IV, 370—cited by Thiessen.

Plutarch:
II, 37—cited by Cooke; II, 97—cited by Cooke; II, 222—cited by Alexander.

Pope, and Moulton:
II, 83—cited by Gerhart.

Priestley, Joseph:
I, 277—cited by Watson; I, 278—cited by Watson; I, 320.

Princell, J. G., Parables of Christ; unpublished ms.:
V, 168.

Pythagoras:
I, 150—cited by Bowne.

# R

Ramsey, Chevalier:
I, 195—cited by Watson.

Randles, Marshall, Substitution:
III, 200.

Rees, T., "God," International Standard Bible Encyclopaedia; Howard-Severance Co., Chicago, 1915:
VII, 174 f., 207.

Rice, W. A., Crusaders of the Twentieth Century:
I, 273—citation of Coquerel; I, 287—citation of Koran; I, 287.

Riddle, M. B., International Revision Commentary, edited by Philip Schaff, Romans; Charles Scribner's Sons, New York, 1883:
II, 301, 308—citation of Besser; II, 310 ff.

Rishell, C. W.:
VII, 198—cited by Hamilton.

Roach, Morris H., The Personality of God; unpublished dissertation, Dallas Theological Seminary, 1933:
I, 223 f.

Robertson, A. T.:
VII, 37.

Robinson, Greek and English Lexicon of New Testament, new ed.:
I, 79.

Rogers, Henry, Superhuman Origin of the Bible, 5th ed.; Hodder & Stoughton, London:
I, 23—citation of Hampden; I, 32—citation of Castenove; I, 36—citation of Parker.

——:
III, 66—cited by Stock.

Rossetti:
II, 4—cited by Strong.

Rothe, Richard:
I, 65—cited by Warfield; IV, 259—cited by Peters; V, 316—cited by Peters as quoted by Auberlen.

Row, C. A.:
II, 127—cited by Laidlaw.

S

Sanger, James Mortimer, The Redeemed, Who Are They?:
III, 189.

Schaff, Philip:
I, 75—cited by Manly; I, 87 f.—cited by Manly; II, 83—cited by Gerhart.

——, Creeds of Christendom; Harper & Bros., New York, 1919:
I, 387.

Schleiermacher:
I, 70.

Schmiedel:
I, 345 f.—cited by Warfield.

Scofield, C. I., Scofield Reference Bible; Oxford University Press, New York:
I, 268 f., 284; II, 17 f., 18 f., 156 f.; III, 28, 32, 75 f., 93 ff., 122 f., 250, 302 f.;
IV, 4, 38, 60, 130 f., 286, 293, 311 f., 316, 357 f., 377, 397 f., 413 f.; V, 43 f.—
cited by Walvoord; V, 54 f., 88, 103, 127 f., 178, 181, 197, 226 f., 236, 303; VI,
86, 201 f.; VII, 11, 30, 58 f., 62, 114 f., 175 f., 177, 269.

——, Correspondence Course; Bible Institute Colportage Association, Chicago:
I, 284—citation of Augustine; IV, 149 f., 151 f.

Seneca:
I, 174—cited by Cooke; I, 198—cited by Cooke.

Shedd, W. G. T., Dogmatic Theology (III Volumes), T. & T. Clark, Edinburgh,
1889:
I, 6, 159 (twice), 193—citation of Charnocke; I, 236 f.—citation of Howe;
I, 393 f.; II, 174, 177, 211 f., 212 f.—citation of Augustine; II, 219, 280, 283,
285 f., 286 ff., 363—citations of Müller and Twesten; III, 59, 179 f., 182,
203 f.; VI, 115—cited by Walvoord; VI, 119—cited by Walvoord.

Sherlock, William:
I, 280 f.—cited by Watson.

Simpson, Carnegie:
II, 271—cited by Mabie.

Smeaton, George, The Doctrine of the Atonement; T. & T. Clark, Edinburgh,
1868:
III, 40 f.

Smith, J. Denham, The Brides of Scripture, 3rd ed.; Pickering & Inglis, Glasgow:
IV, 138 f., 141.

Smith, J. Pye, First Lines of Theology:
II, 221.

——:
I, 285—cited by Alexander; I, 299—cited by Watson; III, 153—cited by Dale.

Socinus, Faustus:
I, 323—cited by Alexander.

Socrates:
I, 49—cited by Dick.

South, Robert:
I, 288—cited by Harris.

Stearns:
II, 297—cited by Thomas.

Stephenson:
V, 374—cited by Peters.

Stock, John, Revealed Theology:
III, 62 f.—citation of Channing; III, 66—citation of Henry Rogers.

Storr:
V, 375 f.—cited by Peters.

Strong, Augustus H., Systematic Theology; A. C. Armstrong & Son, New York, 1899:
I, 6, 131—citation of Calvin; I, 157 f., 176—citation of Carlyle; I, 218 f., 283 f., 284—citation of Joseph Cook; I, 381—cited by Feinberg; II, 4, 8—citation of Milton; II, 17, 195 ff., 259; III, 68, 176 f.

Stuart:
I, 65—cited by Warfield.

Sunday School Times (The), Philadelphia:
VII, 197.

Sweet, Louis Matthews, "Satan," International Standard Bible Encyclopaedia; Howard-Severance Co., Chicago, 1915:
II, 37.

——, "Genealogy of Christ," International Standard Bible Encyclopaedia; Howard-Severance Co., Chicago, 1915:
VII, 166 f.

Swift:
I, 284 f.—cited by Alexander.

# T

Taylor, Frederick G., "The Two Advents of the Saviour," The Sunday School Times; Philadelphia:
IV, 307 ff.

Tennant, Frank Robert, "Agnosticism," Encyclopædia Britannica, 14th ed.; New York:
I, 165.

Terry, M. S.:
VII, 205—cited by Rollin T. Chafer.

Tertullian:
I, 282 f.—cited by Harris; IV, 120 f.

Thaumaturgus, Gregory:
V, 59—cited by Dale.

Thayer, J. H.:
VI, 21—cited by Walvoord.

Thayer-Grimm, Greek-English Lexicon of New Testament; T. & T. Clark, Edinburgh:
I, 79.

——:
IV, 151—cited by Scofield; IV, 370—cited by Thiessen.

Theodorus Mopsuestenus:
I, 182—cited by Cooke.

Thiessen, Henry C., Bibliotheca Sacra; Dallas:
IV, 338, 348 f., 361 ff., 369 ff.

Thomas, W. H. Griffith, Principles of Theology; Longmans, Green & Co., New York, 1930:
I, 6, 131, 182, 302; II, 254 f., 283 f.—citation of Matheson; II, 288, 288 f.—citation of Denney; II, 297—citation of Stearns; II, 356; IV, 89—citation of Godet; VI, 8 f.

——, Commentary on Romans; The Religious Tract Society, London:
II, 300, 306.

——, "Resurrection of Christ," International Standard Bible Encyclopaedia; Howard-Severance Co., Chicago, 1915:
IV, 82 f.

Tregelles:
IV, 348—cited by Thiessen.

Trench, R. C., Notes on the Miracles of Our Lord, 2nd Amer. ed.; D. Appleton & Co., New York, 1857:
V, 174 ff.

——, Notes on the Parables of Our Lord, 9th ed.; D. Appleton & Co., New York, 1856:
V, 167.

——, Synonyms of the Greek New Testament; Kegan Paul, Trench, Trübner & Co., London, 1880:
III, 56.

Trumbull, Henry Clay, The Blood Covenant; Charles Scribner's Sons, New York, 1885:
VII, 54.

Tulloch:
IV, 262—cited by Peters.

Turretin, Francis:
III, 44—cited by Dale.

Twesten, Augustus D.:
II, 363—cited by Shedd.

Tyndale:
I, 79.


## U

Unger, Merrill F., Bibliotheca Sacra; Dallas:
VI, 65, 148 ff., 159 ff.


## V

Valentine, Milton, Christian Theology (II Volumes); Lutheran Publishing Society, Philadelphia, 1906:
I, 160; VI, 115—cited by Walvoord.

Van Oosterzee, J. J., Christian Dogmatics; Scribner, Armstrong & Co., New York, 1874:
I, 182 f., 214—citation of Bruch; I, 256—citation of Lange; I, 314 f., 381 —cited by Feinberg; IV, 423–26.

Van Valkenburg:
V, 375—cited by Peters.

Venema, Hermannus, Institutes of Theology (translated by Alex. W. Brown);
T. & T. Clark, Edinburgh, 1850:
I, 277, 290, 301.

Verne, Jules:
V, 286.

Vincent, Marvin R., Word Studies in the New Testament (IV Volumes); Scribner's, New York, 1887–1890:
I, xii, xiii, 204 f., 205—citation of Godet; I, 254; II, 194—citations of Plato
and Ovid; IV, 38 f., 129; V, 10, 11; VI, 38.

Voltaire:
I, 184—cited by Harris.

Vondel, J., Lucifer (translated by Leonard Charles Van Noppen); Continental
Publishing Co., New York, 1898:
II, 200 ff.

Von Gerlach, Otto:
II, 25—cited by Gerhart.

W

Walch:
IV, 278—cited by Peters.

Waller, C. H., The Authoritative Inspiration of Holy Scripture; Blackie &
Son, London, 1887:
I, 99 f., footnote.

Walvoord, John F., Outline of Christology; unpublished:
V, 12, 31, 43 f., 44 f.

——, The Doctrine of the Holy Spirit; Dallas Theological Seminary, Dallas,
1943:
VI, 19 ff., 49 f., 57–60, 60 ff., 69—citation of A. Kuyper; VI, 75–79, 114–121,
135 f., 218 ff.

Wardlaw, Ralph, Theology (II Volumes); Adams and Charles Black, Edinburgh, 1856:
I, 283—citation of Dick; I, 313 f., 315; III, 269, 286 f.

Warfield, Benjamin B., Bibliotheca Sacra; Oberlin:
I, 62, 70 f.

——, Biblical Doctrines; Oxford University Press, New York, 1929:
I, 371 f., 375, 385 f., 402 f.—citation of Denney; I, 403, 409 f.; IV, 255 f.

Warfield, Benjamin B., Christology and Criticism; Oxford University Press, New York, 1929:
I, 345 f., 395 f.; V, 51 ff.

——, New Schaff-Herzog Encyclopaedia of Religious Knowledge; Funk & Wagnalls Co., New York, 1908:
III, 139 f.; IV, 421 f.

——, "Person of Christ," International Standard Bible Encyclopaedia; Howard-Severance Co., Chicago, 1915:
I, 325, 326 f.; V, 39–42.

——, Princeton Review; Princeton:
VI, 251 f.

——, Revelation and Inspiration; Oxford University Press, New York, 1927:
I, 53, 65—citation of Rothe; I, 65—citation of Stuart; I, 80; IV, 281 f.

——, Studies in Theology; Oxford University Press, New York, 1932:
III, 155–64.

——:
I, 79; VI, 58 f.—cited by Walvoord; VI, 78—cited by Walvoord; VII, 199— cited by Hamilton; VII, 238.

Waterland:
I, 278—cited by Watson; I, 279—cited by Watson.

Watson, Richard, Theological Institutes (II Volumes); Carlton & Phillips, New York, 1856:
I, 135 footnote—citation of Lawson & Newton; I, 143—citation of Leland; I, 144—citation of Dwight; I, 145 f.—citation of Cudworth; I, 146 f.—citation of Paley; I, 147—citation of Locke; I, 147—citation of Howe; I, 147 ff.— citation of Howe; I, 153 f.—citation of Paley; I, 160, 182, 183 f.—citation of Newton; I, 195—citation of Ramsey; I, 195 f., 210—citation of Howe; I, 210 ff., 215—citation of Athanasian Creed; I, 268, 277—citation of Priestley; I, 278—citation of Waterland; I, 278 f.—citation of Priestley; I, 279—citation of Waterland; I, 279 f., 280—citation of Graves; I, 280 f.—citation of Sherlock; I, 281 f., 289—citation of Baxter; I, 299—citation of J. Pye Smith; I, 300 f., 323 f.—citation of Whitaker; I, 331, 346 f., 351—citation of Athanasian and Anglican Creeds; I, 366, 399 ff.; II, 162—citation of Howe; II, 163, 163 f. —citation of Watts; II, 164—citation of Edwards; II, 164 ff., 204—citation of Horsley; II, 206 ff., 208, 208 f.—citation of King; II, 212—citation of Butler; II, 281; III, 182—cited by Shedd; VI, 10—citations of Nicene Creed and Thirty-Nine Articles; VII, 199.

Watts, Isaac:
II, 163 f.—cited by Watson.

Webster, J. H., "Pauline Theology," International Standard Bible Encyclopaedia; Howard-Severance Co., Chicago, 1915:
VII, 249.

Weiss:
VII, 159—cited by Hodge.

Werner, H.:
V, 52—cited by Warfield.

Wesley, Charles:
V, 3.

Wesley, John:
II, 275.

Westcott, and Hort:
I, 87—cited by Manly; IV, 370—cited by Thiessen.

Whitaker, John:
I, 323 f.—cited by Watson.

Whitby, Daniel:
IV, 275—cited by Peters; V, 286 ff.; VII, 237.

Williams, Daniel:
III, 70 f.—cited by Alexander.

Wilson, R.:
V, 68—cited by Dale.

Winchester, A. B., God Hath Spoken; Bible Conference Committee, Philadelphia, 1919:
I, 339 f.

Witsius:
II, 69—cited by Alexander.

Wolf, Abraham, "Intelligence," Encyclopædia Britannica, 14th ed.; New York:
II, 193.

Wollaston:
I, 146—cited by Cooke.

Wycliff:
I, 79.

## CATECHISMS, CREEDS, DICTIONARIES, AND ENCYCLOPAEDIAS

Athanasian Creed:
I, 215—cited by Watson; I, 283—cited by Harris; I, 285—cited by Alexander;
I, 351—cited by Watson; I, 400—cited by Watson.

Augsburg Confession:
IV, 279—from Müller, cited by Peters.

Chalcedonian Symbol:
I, 386 f.—in Schaff, cited by Miley.

Creed of the Church of England:
I, 351—cited by Watson; I, 400—cited by Watson.

Didache of the Apostles:
IV, 121.

Encyclopædia Britannica, 14th ed.; Encyclopædia Britannica, Inc., New York:
I, 159, 171; II, 174, 195; IV, 156, 264.
(For quotations from signed articles, see name of author of article.)

Epistle of Barnabas:
III, 136.

Epistle to Diognetus:
III, 136—cited by Dale.

Evangelium Infantiœ:
V, 173.

Formula Consensus Helvetica:
III, 69—cited by Alexander.

International Standard Bible Encyclopaedia; Howard-Severance Co., Chicago,
1915. Now published by Wm. B. Eerdmans Publishing Co., Grand Rapids:
V, 45—cited by Walvoord; VI, 50—cited by Walvoord; VII, 249.
(For quotations from signed articles, see name of author of article.)

Jackson, J. B., Dictionary of Scripture Proper Names; Loizeaux Bros., New
York, 1909:
I, 265.

Koran:
I, 287—cited by Rice.

New Century Dictionary, 1936 ed.; D. Appleton–Century Co., New York:
I, 168.

New Standard Dictionary, 1913 ed.; Funk & Wagnalls Co., New York:
I, 158, 171, 172 f., 177 (twice), 178, 217, 251, 382; II, 126, 279; III, 127; VII, 17, 18.

Nicene Creed:
I, 285—cited by Alexander; I, 316—cited by Hodge; I, 400—cited by Watson; VI, 10—cited by Watson.

Smith's Comprehensive Dictionary of the Bible, edited by Samuel W. Barnum; D. Appleton & Co., New York, 1901:
II, 17.

Thirty-Nine Articles:
VI, 10—cited by Watson.

Westminster Confession of Faith:
I, 188 f., 225, 248, 387; III, 192, 267; V, 7 f.; VI, 10.

Westminster Larger Catechism:
I, 283—cited by Harris; II, 227, 262; VII, 173.

Westminster Shorter Catechism:
I, 228; II, 275; VII, 219.

# SCRIPTURE INDEX

# SCRIPTURE INDEX

This index of Scripture references is limited to passages concerning which some interpretative comment is made. Listings of Scripture references as proof texts, quotation of passages for the same purpose, and allusions to Scripture are not included.

## GENESIS

| | |
|---|---|
| 1:1 | I, 306, 403 f. |
| 1:2 | VI, 27, 66 f. |
| 1:26 | II, 166 |
| 1:26–27 | I, 266; II, 135 f., 167 |
| 2:7 | II, 144 |
| 2:17 | II, 345 f. |
| 3:1 | II, 203 |
| 3:1–7 | II, 209 f. |
| 3:1–19 | II, 249 ff. |
| 3:5 | I, 239, 267 |
| 3:15 | II, 117; III, 125 f., 189; IV, 302, 345 f.; V, 185 f. |
| 3:21 | III, 124 |
| 4:4 | III, 119 |
| 6:3 | VI, 28, 68 |
| 6:6 | I, 218 |
| 8:20–22 | III, 119 |
| 8:21 | II, 289 |
| 11:6–9 | VI, 17 |
| 12:3 | IV, 410 |
| 14:17–24 | III, 124 |
| 14:18 | V, 235 |
| 18:19 | IV, 157 |
| 22:1–14 | III, 124 |
| 26:5 | II, 260 f.; IV, 157 f. |

## EXODUS

| | |
|---|---|
| 3:14 | I, 263 |
| 6:3 | I, 262 f. |
| 12:3, 6 | III, 37 |
| 16:14–22 | III, 125 |
| 17:5–7 | III, 125 |
| 19:3–8 | IV, 162 f. |
| 21:1–6 | III, 89 f. |
| 25:6 | VI, 49 |
| 30:17–21 | II, 341 |

## LEVITICUS

| | |
|---|---|
| 2:1 | VI, 48 |
| 2:4–5 | VI, 48 |
| 2:7 | VI, 48 |
| 11:44 | VII, 188 |
| 14:1–7 | III, 122 |
| 14:4–7 | V, 235 f. |
| 23:10–11 | V, 236 |
| 25:25–57 | I, 362 |

## NUMBERS

| | |
|---|---|
| 6:24–26 | I, 308 f.; VI, 18 |
| 6:24–27 | I, 299 |
| 17:8 | V, 236 |
| 19:1–22 | II, 341 |
| 20:7–13 | III, 125 |
| 23:21 | II, 59 f. |

## DEUTERONOMY

| | |
|---|---|
| 4:2 | I, 98 |
| 6:4 | I, 266 f.; VI, 17; VII, 174, 208 |
| 18:15, 18–19 | I, 100, 356 f.; III, 19, 20 f. |
| 30:1–8 | V, 289 ff. |
| 30:3 | V, 28 |

## I SAMUEL

| | |
|---|---|
| 16:14 | VI, 129 f. |
| 28:7–14 | II, 118 |

## II SAMUEL

| | |
|---|---|
| 7:16 | I, 360 |

## JOB

| | |
|---|---|
| 1:9 | II, 73 |
| 9:32–33 | III, 61 |
| 20:4–5 | II, 205 |
| 26:13 | VI, 68 |
| 27:3 | VI, 69 |
| 33:4 | I, 398; VI, 69 |

## PSALMS

| | |
|---|---|
| 2:1–3 | II, 69 |
| 2:1–12 | IV, 342 |
| 2:6–9 | V, 291 f. |
| 8:1–9 | V, 135 f. |
| 8:3 | III, 52 |
| 8:5 | II, 168 |
| 16:9–10 | V, 236 f. |
| 22:4–5 | V, 183 |
| 22:6–8 | V, 183 f. |
| 22:22–31 | V, 237 |
| 40:6 | VI, 261 |
| 40:6–8 | III, 90 |
| 45:8–15 | V, 132 |

| | |
|---|---|
| 51:1–19 | VI, 243 f. |
| 51:5 | II, 290 |
| 51:11 | VI, 71, 130 |
| 96:11–13 | I, 331 |
| 98:7–9 | I, 331 |
| 118:22–24 | IV, 115 f.; V, 237 f. |
| 138:1 | I, 267 |

## ECCLESIASTES

| | |
|---|---|
| 12:1 | I, 301; VI, 17 |

## ISAIAH

| | |
|---|---|
| 6:3 | I, 304; VI, 17 f. |
| 6:9–10 | I, 105 |
| 6:10 | I, 240 |
| 7:14 | I, 351 |
| 9:2 | I, 107 |
| 9:6 | III, 31 |
| 9:6–7 | I, 334, 351 f.; V, 29, 323 f. |
| 11:1–4 | I, 406 |
| 13:1–22 | IV, 357 f. |
| 14:12–14 | I, 239; II, 64, 246 ff. |
| 14:12–17 | II, 44–50 |
| 14:13–14 | VI, 256 |
| 32:15 | I, 408 |
| 40:1–2 | IV, 290 |
| 40:1–3 | V, 30 |
| 40:3 | I, 334; V, 12 |
| 44:3 | I, 408 |
| 50:6 | V, 186 |
| 52:13—53:12 | V, 184 f. |
| 53:1 | III, 52 |
| 53:4 | III, 39 |
| 53:5 | III, 38 f.n.; VII, 184 |
| 54:5 | I, 301 |
| 55:6 | III, 389 |
| 59:20 | V, 300 f. |
| 59:21 | I, 408 |
| 60:1–5 | V, 300 f. |
| 61:1–3 | I, 407; IV, 303 |

| | | | |
|---|---|---|---|
| 63:1–6 | IV, 342; V, 292 f. | JOEL | |
| 63:2–3 | VI, 139 | 2:28–29 | I, 407 |
| 65:20 | II, 314 f. | | |

**MICAH**

| | |
|---|---|
| 5:2 | I, 352 |

**JEREMIAH**

| | |
|---|---|
| 17:5, 9 | II, 290 |
| 23:5–6 | I, 333; V, 30 f., 324 |
| 33:14–17 | V, 29 |
| 33:14–26 | I, 361 |

**ZECHARIAH**

| | |
|---|---|
| 1:4, 9, 16 | V, 30 |
| 9:9 | V, 29 f. |
| 12:10 | I, 333, 409; V, 126, 186 f. |
| 13:6–7 | V, 186 f. |
| 14:1–4 | V, 295 f. |

**EZEKIEL**

| | |
|---|---|
| 20:33–44 | IV, 407 f. |
| 28:1–10 | II, 40; IV, 347 f. |
| 28:11–12 | II, 40 f. |
| 28:11–15 | II, 243 ff. |
| 28:11–19 | II, 39–44 |
| 28:13 | II, 41 f. |
| 28:14 | II, 42 |
| 28:15 | II, 42 f. |
| 28:16 | II, 43 |
| 28:17 | II, 43, 63 f. |
| 28:18–19 | II, 43 f. |
| 33:7–8 | III, 293 |
| 37:21–28 | V, 324 f. |

**MALACHI**

| | |
|---|---|
| 3:1 | I, 329; IV, 304 |
| 3:1–3 | V, 302 f. |
| 3:1–6 | IV, 408 |

**MATTHEW**

| | |
|---|---|
| 1:1 | V, 326 |
| 1:23 | I, 335; V, 13 |
| 3:1–2 | IV, 294; V, 66 f. |
| 3:2 | VII, 266 |
| 3:6 | V, 67; VII, 40 |
| 3:11 | V, 67 |
| 3:15 | V, 60–63 |
| 3:16 | VII, 40 |
| 3:17 | I, 357 |
| 5:1–12 | IV, 216–19 |
| 5:1—7:29 | III, 23 f. |
| 5:3–12 | V, 103 ff. |
| 5:13–16 | IV, 219; V, 105 |
| 5:17–48 | IV, 219 ff.; V, 105–8 |
| 6:1–18 | V, 108 f. |
| 6:8–15 | IV, 221 |
| 6:13 | V, 74 |
| 6:14–15 | II, 339 f. |

**DANIEL**

| | |
|---|---|
| 2:1–49 | IV, 332–35 |
| 2:34–35 | V, 294 f. |
| 7:1–28 | IV, 235 ff. |
| 7:13–14 | V, 301 f., 325 f. |
| 9:1–27 | IV, 337–41 |
| 9:27 | IV, 348 f. |
| 12:1 | II, 20 |
| 12:2 | II, 149 |
| 12:2–3 | IV, 407 |

**HOSEA**

| | |
|---|---|
| 3:4–5 | V, 326 |

MATTHEW (*continued*)

| | |
|---|---|
| 6:19–24 | V, 109 |
| 6:25–34 | IV, 222 f.; V, 109 f. |
| 7:1–6 | V, 110 |
| 7:7–11 | V, 110 |
| 7:12 | VII, 164 f. |
| 7:12–14 | V, 110 f. |
| 7:13–14 | IV, 224 |
| 7:15–29 | V, 111 |
| 7:24 | IV, 225; VII, 184 |
| 8:16–17 | III, 39 |
| 10:8 | VII, 184 |
| 10:32 | III, 379 |
| 11:10–11 | IV, 292 f. |
| 11:27–28 | VI, 107 |
| 12:29 | II, 113 |
| 12:31–32 | VII, 47 f. |
| 13:1–8 | III, 296 |
| 13:1–58 | IV, 55, 352 f.; V, 349–53 |
| 13:11 | V, 349; VII, 224 |
| 13:38–40 | VII, 121 f. |
| 13:44 | IV, 386 |
| 16:18 | IV, 43 |
| 16:27—17:13 | V, 86–94 |
| 16:28 | VII, 305 f. |
| 16:28—17:8 | I, 117 |
| 17:5 | I, 357 |
| 18:23–35 | III, 292 f. |
| 20:22 | V, 72 f. |
| 21:1–10 | I, 330 |
| 21:42–44 | IV, 62 f. |
| 23:37–39 | V, 116 ff. |
| 24:1–3 | V, 118 ff. |
| 24:1—25:46 | III, 24 f. |
| 24:3 | VII, 122 |
| 24:4–8 | V, 120 |
| 24:9–28 | V, 120–25 |
| 24:13 | III, 292 |
| 24:14 | V, 282 |
| 24:22 | IV, 369 |
| 24:29 | VII, 14 |
| 24:29–31 | IV, 319; V, 125 f., 135 |
| 24:31 | II, 24 |
| 24:32–36 | V, 126 ff. |
| 24:34 | IV, 316; V, 285 |
| 24:37–39 | V, 129 |
| 24:37—25:13 | V, 128–33 |
| 24:37—25:30 | IV, 132 f.; IV, 408 f. |
| 24:40–42 | V, 129 f. |
| 24:45–51 | V, 130 |
| 25:1–13 | III, 302; IV, 131 f.; V, 131 ff. |
| 25:10 | V, 131 f.; VII, 61 |
| 25:14–30 | V, 133 f. |
| 25:31–46 | III, 170; IV, 5 f., 343; V, 134–40 |
| 27:63–64 | V, 240 |
| 28:9 | V, 238 |
| 28:18–20 | VI, 9 |
| 28:19 | I, 303 f. |

MARK

| | |
|---|---|
| 1:4–5 | V, 67 |
| 1:9 | V, 67 ff. |
| 3:28–30 | VII, 47 f. |
| 9:1–9 | V, 303 ff. |
| 9:1–13 | V, 86–94 |
| 10:38–39 | V, 72 f. |
| 16:15–16 | III, 381 ff. |
| 16:16 | VI, 150 |

LUKE

| | |
|---|---|
| 1:30–33 | IV, 304 |
| 1:30–35 | I, 352 |
| 1:31–32 | V, 326 f. |
| 1:31–33 | V, 341 |
| 3:3 | V, 67 |
| 4:1–13 | II, 51 f.; V, 79 f. |
| 4:5–7 | II, 80 f. |
| 4:18–19 | IV, 303 |
| 9:27–36 | V, 86–94 |
| 10:18 | II, 45 f. |
| 11:1 | V, 160 f. |

| | | | |
|---|---|---|---|
| 11:13 | VI, 72, 130 f. | 3:3 | III, 215 f. |
| 11:24–26 | III, 295 f. | 3:5 | I, 122 |
| 12:35–36 | IV, 396 | 3:14 | V, 192 f. |
| 12:35–40 | V, 305 f. | 3:16 | II, 78; III, 7 f., |
| 12:50 | V, 72 f. | | 394 ff.; VI. |
| 13:24 | IV, 224 | | 113 f. |
| 15:1–2 | VI, 245 f. | 3:22–23 | V, 67 |
| 15:1–32 | III, 230; VI, | 3:23 | VII, 39 |
| | 244–49 | 3:29 | IV, 129 |
| 15:3–7 | VI, 246 f. | 4:14 | VI, 51 |
| 15:8–10 | VI, 247 | 5:19 | III, 22 |
| 15:10 | II, 26 | 5:22 | I, 336 |
| 15:11–32 | VI, 247 ff. | 5:25–29 | IV, 375 |
| 16:16 | IV, 214 f. | 6:33, 38, 41, | |
| 17:20–21 | IV, 178 | 50–51, 58, | |
| 17:21 | V, 339, 343 | 62 | I, 322 f.; V, 34 |
| 18:13 | III, 95, 390 ff.; | 6:39–40 | VI, 90 f. |
| | VII, 259 f. | 6:44 | III, 216; VI, 91; |
| 19:11 | IV, 368 | | VII, 65 |
| 22:19–20 | III, 57 | 6:51 | III, 57; V, 193 |
| 22:31 | II, 46 | 6:63 | III, 22 |
| 22:31–34 | III, 332 f. | 7:37–39 | IV, 192; VI, |
| 22:67–71 | I, 335 | | 124 f. |
| 24:27–32, 45 | I, 9 | 8:24 | III, 196 f. |
| 24:37–39 | II, 12 | 8:31 | III, 297 |
| 24:39 | IV, 118; VII, 20 | 8:37–39 | IV, 312 |
| 24:47 | III, 377 | 8:44 | II, 64–68 |
| | | 8:56–59 | I, 264 |
| | | 8:58 | I, 323, 341 |
| **JOHN** | | 8:58–59 | V, 34 f. |
| | | 10:1–42 | IV, 57 |
| 1:1 | VII, 195 | 10:11 | V, 194 |
| 1:1–2 | I, 297; III, 12– | 10:15 | III, 201 |
| | 15 | 10:34–35 | I, 83 |
| 1:1–2, 14 | I, 58, 352 | 10:40 | V, 67 |
| 1:1–4, 14 | I, 324 f.; V, 33 f. | 11:25 | IV, 96 |
| 1:3, 10 | I, 342 | 11:49–52 | V, 194 f. |
| 1:12 | VII, 75 | 12:24 | V, 195 f. |
| 1:12–13 | VI, 113 | 12:32 | VII, 65 |
| 1:14 | III, 12–15 | 13:1 | VI, 204; VII, 231 |
| 1:15, 30 | I, 322 | 13:1–17 | II, 241 |
| 1:16–17 | IV, 240; V, 191 | 13:1—17:26 | III, 25 f. |
| 1:18 | VII, 228 | 13:3–11 | VI, 236 ff. |
| 1:19–28 | V, 58 | 13:4–10 | V, 147 f. |
| 1:29 | V, 189 ff. | 13:8 | III, 309 |
| 1:32–33 | V, 71 f. | 13:34 | IV, 187 f. |
| 2:19 | VI, 23 f. | 14:1–3 | V, 164 f., 277 f. |

JOHN (*continued*)
| | |
|---|---|
| 14:2 | II, 7 |
| 14:6 | I, 97; II, 68 |
| 14:12–14 | V, 161 ff.; VII, 253 |
| 14:16–17 | V, 151 f.; VI, 72, 90, 125 f. VII, 11 f. |
| 14:20 | III, 72 f., 244; V, 144 |
| 14:25–26 | I, 85 |
| 14:27 | VI, 208 |
| 15:1–10 | V, 149 ff. |
| 15:1–16 | VI, 258 |
| 15:1–27 | IV, 59 ff. |
| 15:2 | III, 299, 309; V, 149 f.; VI, 164, 242; VII, 4 |
| 15:5 | VII, 6 |
| 15:6 | III, 298 ff.; VII, 4 f. |
| 15:7 | V, 163 f. |
| 15:10 | V, 149; VII, 5 f. |
| 15:12 | IV, 187 f. |
| 15:13 | III, 57; V, 196 f. |
| 15:25 | IV, 242 f. |
| 15:26–27 | I, 85 |
| 16:7–11 | I, 412; III, 217–23; V, 152 ff.; VI, 33 f., 93–98; VII, 94 ff. |
| 16:12–13 | V, 275 |
| 16:12–15 | I, 85, 110; V, 154–57; VI, 222 ff. |
| 16:13 | VI, 37 |
| 16:23 | VII, 253 |
| 16:23–24 | V, 164 |
| 16:24 | V, 109 |
| 17:1–26 | III, 332 |
| 17:4 | III, 87 |
| 17:5 | I, 296, 326; V, 35 f. |
| 17:11 | III, 324; V, 157 f. |
| 17:20 | V, 145 |
| 17:21–23 | III, 254; V, 158 ff.; VI, 153 f. |
| 18:37 | I, 97, 361 |
| 20:17 | IV, 118; V, 262 f.; VII, 20 |
| 20:22 | I, 398 |

ACTS

| | |
|---|---|
| 1:6–7 | IV, 266 |
| 1:8 | IV, 192 |
| 1:9–11 | V, 272 f., 299 f. |
| 2:25–31 | V, 327 f. |
| 2:30–31 | II, 188 |
| 2:38 | III, 383 |
| 3:21 | IV, 423 |
| 4:10–11 | IV, 85, 116 |
| 5:32 | VI, 131 |
| 8:14–20 | VI, 131 f. |
| 8:38 | VII, 40 |
| 8:39 | VII, 40 |
| 9:18 | VII, 41 |
| 11:17 | VI, 126 |
| 11:18 | III, 377 |
| 15:10 | III, 82; V, 75 |
| 15:13–18 | IV, 268 f.; V, 279, 328 f. |
| 15:16–18 | V, 300 |
| 15:17 | IV, 416 |
| 17:30 | III, 104 |
| 19:1–6 | VI, 132 f. |
| 20:21 | III, 377 f. |
| 26:20 | III, 378 |

ROMANS

| | |
|---|---|
| 1:16–17 | III, 82 f. |
| 2:12 | IV, 237 |
| 2:12–16 | I, 204 |
| 2:13 | IV, 239 |
| 2:14–15 | IV, 237 f. |
| 2:25 | IV, 239 |
| 3:9 | III, 231 |

| | | | |
|---|---|---|---|
| 3:10–12 | III, 78 | 6:3–6 | V, 204 f. |
| 3:10–18 | III, 213 | 6:6 | II, 157 f., 348; |
| 3:21–22 | III, 83 | | VI, 269 |
| 3:22–24 | VII, 221 f. | 6:10 | III, 97; V, 205 |
| 3:23–26 | V, 201 ff. | 6:11–12 | V, 205 f. |
| 3:25 | III, 104 f. | 6:11–13 | VI, 275 f. |
| 3:31 | III, 83; IV, | 6:14 | IV, 192, 240 |
| | 239 f. | 7:2–6 | IV, 240 f. |
| 4:5 | III, 83, 201 | 7:4 | IV, 129 |
| 4:11 | III, 83 f. | 7:4–6 | V, 206 |
| 4:13–16 | III, 84 | 7:6 | I, 398; VI, 123 |
| 4:13–24 | IV, 235 | 7:15–24 | II, 354 f.; VI, |
| 4:14 | IV, 239 | | 272 ff. |
| 4:16 | III, 229, 318 f. | 7:15–25 | VI, 186 ff. |
| 4:23–24 | III, 84 | 7:16 | IV, 240 |
| 4:25 | II, 274; IV, 88; | 7:18 | II, 189 |
| | V, 203 f., | 7:24 | II, 158 |
| | 248 f.; VII, | 8:1 | III, 340 ff. |
| | 222 | 8:2 | II, 355 |
| 5:1 | VI, 208 | 8:2–8 | III, 342–45 |
| 5:5 | VI, 126, 203; | 8:3 | VII, 156 f. |
| | VII, 230 | 8:3–4 | II, 355; V, 206 f. |
| 5:6–8 | III, 57 | 8:4 | IV, 192 |
| 5:6–10 | V, 204 | 8:5–13 | II, 190 |
| 5:7 | VI, 211 | 8:9 | VI, 126 f. |
| 5:10–11 | III, 93 | 8:9–13 | III, 345 f. |
| 5:12 | II, 154, 243, | 8:12–13 | II, 356 |
| | 300–4; VII, | 8:13–14 | VII, 70 |
| | 192 | 8:14 | VI, 225 |
| 5:12–14 | VII, 113 | 8:14–17 | III, 346 f. |
| 5:12–21 | II, 299–310; | 8:16–17 | VI, 110 |
| | VII, 7 f. | 8:23 | VI, 127 |
| 5:13 | IV, 158 | 8:26–27 | VII, 202, 254 |
| 5:13–14 | II, 304 f. | 8:28–29 | III, 347 f. |
| 5:15–19 | II, 305 ff. | 8:28–30 | III, 317; VI, |
| 5:19 | III, 84 | | 91 ff., 112 |
| 5:20 | II, 307 f. | 8:29–30 | VII, 66 f. |
| 5:21 | II, 308 ff. | 8:30 | III, 175 |
| 6:1–4 | VI, 144 f. | 8:30–33 | III, 349 ff. |
| 6:1–10 | III, 240; VI, | 8:32 | III, 57; V, 207 |
| | 190 ff., 276– | 8:34 | III, 332, 351; |
| | 82; VII, 36 | | V, 207 f. |
| 6:1–14 | II, 351–54 | 8:35–39 | III, 351–54 |
| 6:1—8:13 | III, 98–101 | 9:1–3 | VI, 205; VII, |
| 6:2–4 | VII, 63 f. | | 232 |
| 6:2–5 | IV, 96 | 9:6 | III, 4 |

## II CORINTHIANS

| | |
|---|---|
| 1:3 | VII, 151 |
| 1:21–22 | III, 338; VI, 133 |
| 1:22 | VI, 136 |
| 3:6 | I, 398; IV, 190; VI, 123 |
| 3:7–13 | IV, 241 f. |
| 3:9 | II, 316 |
| 3:17 | I, 399 |
| 3:18 | V, 86 |
| 4:3–4 | I, 107; II, 324; III, 214; V, 153 f.; VI, 90 |
| 4:4 | V, 350 |
| 4:10–11 | VII, 106 |
| 5:1–5 | IV, 414 |
| 5:1–8 | II, 156; VII, 56 f. |
| 5:5 | VI, 128 f. |
| 5:9–10 | IV, 406 |
| 5:10 | IV, 377; VII, 215 |
| 5:14 | III, 57 |
| 5:14–16 | IV, 197 |
| 5:14–21 | V, 209 ff. |
| 5:16 | VI, 207 |
| 5:17 | V, 248 |
| 5:17–18 | II, 322; IV, 94; V, 257; VII, 220 |
| 5:17–20 | VII, 262 f. |
| 5:19–20 | III, 91 ff. |
| 5:21 | III, 49, 57, 84 f. |
| 7:8–11 | VI, 243 |
| 7:10 | III, 372 |
| 8:9 | V, 211 |
| 10:3–5 | IV, 193 |
| 11:2 | IV, 129 |
| 11:13–15 | II, 107 f. |
| 11:15 | II, 59 |
| 13:14 | VI, 18 |

## GALATIANS

| | |
|---|---|
| 1:4 | V, 212, 350 |
| 2:20 | V, 212 |
| 3:2 | VI, 129 |
| 3:8 | I, 84; III, 85 |
| 3:13 | III, 57; V, 212 f. |
| 3:14 | IV, 229 |
| 3:19 | IV, 161 |
| 3:22 | II, 318; III, 231; IV, 235 f. |
| 3:22–25 | IV, 165 |
| 3:23 | IV, 239 |
| 3:27 | VI, 143 f. |
| 3:27–28 | IV, 94 |
| 4:4–5 | V, 213 ff. |
| 4:6 | VI, 129 |
| 4:9 | IV, 161 f. |
| 4:9–10 | IV, 110 f. |
| 4:19–31 | III, 85; IV, 129 f. |
| 4:21–31 | IV, 230 f. |
| 5:1 | III, 85 f., 241; VII, 10 |
| 5:4 | III, 310 f. |
| 5:16 | II, 331; IV, 193; VI, 261 f. |
| 5:16–17 | II, 356; VI, 186 |
| 5:17–21 | II, 291; VI, 199 f. |
| 5:18 | IV, 242; VI, 123, 171, 262 f. |
| 5:22 | VI, 24 f., 212 |
| 5:22–23 | III, 361 f.; IV, 193 f., 219; VI, 201–15 |
| 5:23 | VI, 214 |
| 5:24 | VI, 190 |
| 6:14 | V, 212 |
| 6:15 | IV, 94 |
| 6:16 | IV, 313 |

## EPHESIANS

| | |
|---|---|
| 1:3 | III, 265 |
| 1:4–5 | III, 242 f., 321 f. |
| 1:7 | V, 215 f. |
| 1:13 | VI, 133, 136 |
| 1:13–14 | III, 338 f. |
| 1:19–21 | V, 250 ff. |

EPHESIANS (*continued*)

| | |
|---|---|
| 1:20–23 | V, 272 |
| 2:1 | VI, 90 |
| 2:1–2 | II, 217, 323; III, 247 |
| 2:1–3 | III, 214 f. |
| 2:1–22 | IV, 72–75 |
| 2:2 | I, 240 |
| 2:4–5 | I, 206 f.; VII, 178 |
| 2:4–6 | IV, 97 |
| 2:7 | III, 8, 228 f.; IV, 182 |
| 2:8–9 | III, 216 f. |
| 2:8–10 | III, 7 |
| 2:10 | IV, 94 f. |
| 2:13 | V, 216 ff. |
| 2:14–18 | III, 112 |
| 2:15 | IV, 95 |
| 2:19–20 | III, 20 |
| 2:20 | I, 101 |
| 3:1–21 | IV, 75 ff. |
| 3:18–19 | IV, 133 f. |
| 4:1–6 | V, 159 |
| 4:4–6 | VI, 146 ff. |
| 4:5 | VII, 36 |
| 4:8–10 | V, 272 |
| 4:11 | III, 19 f.; VI, 217 f.; VII, 145 f. |
| 4:11–12 | I, ix; IV, 68 f. |
| 4:13–16 | IV, 70 |
| 4:20–24 | VI, 193 f. |
| 4:21–24 | IV, 95 |
| 4:22–24 | VI, 270 |
| 4:30 | III, 339; VI, 136 f., 234 f. |
| 4:32 | II, 339 |
| 5:1–2 | V, 218 f. |
| 5:2, 25 | III, 57 |
| 5:6 | III, 197 |
| 5:8 | III, 262 |
| 5:25–27 | V, 219 f. |
| 5:25–33 | IV, 130 f. |
| 6:2 | IV, 210 |
| 6:10–11 | IV, 193 |
| 6:10–12 | VI, 267 |
| 6:10–17 | VI, 194 f. |
| 6:12 | II, 81 |
| 6:16 | VI, 268 |

PHILIPPIANS

| | |
|---|---|
| 2:4 | I, 374 f. |
| 2:5 | I, 375; VI, 257 |
| 2:5–8 | I, 373 f. |
| 2:6 | I, 325, 375 ff.; V, 36 ff. |
| 2:6–8 | I, 352 f. |
| 2:6–11 | VI, 257 f. |
| 2:7 | I, 378 f. |
| 2:8 | V, 220 |
| 2:10–11 | IV, 423 |
| 2:12 | III, 312 |
| 2:13 | I, 240; IV, 193; VI, 195 f. |
| 3:10 | V, 220 f. |
| 3:21 | II, 158 |
| 4:17 | VI, 208 |

COLOSSIANS

| | |
|---|---|
| 1:12 | VI, 154 |
| 1:13 | II, 323 |
| 1:13–17 | I, 353 |
| 1:15 | V, 11–12 |
| 1:15–18 | II, 53 f. |
| 1:15–19 | V, 24–27 |
| 1:16–17 | II, 11 |
| 1:20 | IV, 423 |
| 1:20–23 | V, 221 ff. |
| 1:21–23 | III, 307 f. |
| 2:6 | IV, 193 |
| 2:9–10 | III, 264 f. |
| 2:9–13 | VI, 145 f. |
| 2:11 | III, 250 f. |
| 2:11–12 | VI, 192 f.; VII, 63 f. |
| 2:11–13 | VII, 36 |
| 2:13 | III, 238 |
| 2:14–15 | II, 54–57; III, 110 f., 221 f. |
| 2:15 | VI, 98 |

| | |
|---|---|
| 2:16–17 | IV, 109 f. |
| 3:8–10 | VI, 193 f. |
| 3:9–10 | II, 348; VI, 270 |
| 3:13 | II, 339 |

**I THESSALONIANS**

| | |
|---|---|
| 1:9 | III, 374 |
| 1:10 | V, 223 |
| 4:16 | II, 151 |
| 5:9–10 | V, 223 |
| 5:19 | VI, 250 f., 253 |

**II THESSALONIANS**

| | |
|---|---|
| 2:1–12 | II, 69–72 |
| 2:3 | IV, 353 |
| 2:3–10 | VI, 86 ff.; VII, 17 |
| 2:4 | II, 93 |
| 2:4–10 | IV, 349 f. |
| 2:6–7 | I, 412; IV, 372 f. |
| 2:6–8 | VI, 35 |
| 2:7–10 | V, 293 |
| 2:8–12 | V, 296 f. |
| 2:11 | I, 241 |
| 2:13–14 | III, 173 |

**I TIMOTHY**

| | |
|---|---|
| 2:5 | VII, 235 |
| 2:5–6 | III, 57; V, 223 f. |
| 3:6 | II, 63 |
| 3:16 | I, 353; III, 21 ff. |
| 4:1 | I, 102 |
| 4:1–2 | II, 106 f.; III, 293 f. |
| 4:1–3 | II, 117 f. |
| 5:6 | II, 217 |
| 5:8 | III, 311 |
| 5:21 | II, 17 |
| 6:10 | III, 311 |
| 6:16 | V, 245; VII, 153 f. |

**II TIMOTHY**

| | |
|---|---|
| 1:10 | V, 245 |
| 2:18–19 | III, 174 f. |
| 2:20–21 | III, 253 |
| 2:21 | VII, 278 |
| 3:1–5 | II, 105 f. |
| 3:7 | VI, 222 |
| 3:16 | I, 22; VI, 32; VII, 200 f. |
| 3:16–17 | I, 77 ff.; VI, 266 |
| 4:10 | V, 350 |

**TITUS**

| | |
|---|---|
| 2:11–14 | IV, 182 f. |
| 2:14 | V, 224 |
| 3:5 | III, 241 f. |

**PHILEMON**

| | |
|---|---|
| 1:13 | III, 57 |
| 1:17–18 | II, 296 |

**HEBREWS**

| | |
|---|---|
| 1:1–2 | VII, 121 |
| 1:2 | I, xii f., 254 f. |
| 1:2–4 | I, 315 |
| 1:3 | I, 276 |
| 2:9 | III, 57 |
| 2:9–18 | V, 226 f. |
| 3:6, 14 | III, 296 f. |
| 4:4 | IV, 110 |
| 4:12 | I, 120 f.; VII, 45 |
| 4:15 | I, 393; III, 37; V, 82 f. |
| 6:4–9 | III, 302 f.; VII, 95 |
| 6:9 | III, 226 |
| 7:9–10 | II, 303 |
| 7:23–25 | III, 333 f. |
| 7:25 | V, 276 |
| 7:27 | V, 227 f. |

HEBREWS (*continued*)

| | |
|---|---|
| 9:13–14 | VII, 53 |
| 9:14 | VI, 23; VII, 276 |
| 9:16–18 | IV, 118 |
| 9:22 | VII, 53 |
| 9:22–23 | VII, 54 |
| 9:23–24 | V, 264–67 |
| 10:1–2 | II, 198 |
| 10:1–37 | V, 228 f. |
| 10:2 | VII, 22 |
| 10:4–7 | I, 390 |
| 10:5 | I, 358 |
| 10:5–7 | II, 277; III, 90; V, 81 |
| 10:10 | V, 227 f. |
| 10:12 | V, 227 f. |
| 10:13 | V, 278 |
| 10:14 | V, 232; VI, 283 |
| 10:26–29 | III, 303 ff. |
| 11:3 | I, xii f., 254 f.; VII, 100 |
| 12:1–2 | II, 268 |
| 12:2 | V, 227 f. |
| 12:3–4 | V, 83 f. |
| 12:3–15 | IV, 404 |
| 12:5–11 | VI, 241 ff. |
| 12:6 | VII, 72 |
| 12:22–24 | II, 369; IV, 131, 419; V, 366 f. |
| 13:2 | II, 12 |

JAMES

| | |
|---|---|
| 2:5 | II, 87 |
| 2:14–26 | III, 297 |
| 3:17 | VI, 210 |
| 4:4 | VI, 180 |
| 4:7 | VI, 267 |

I PETER

| | |
|---|---|
| 1:16 | VII, 188 |
| 1:18–19 | V, 224 f. |
| 1:20 | III, 37 |
| 1:24–25 | II, 188 |
| 2:9 | III, 251 f.; V, 257 |
| 2:24 | III, 38 f.n.; V, 225 |
| 3:18 | III, 57; V, 225; VI, 23 |
| 3:21 | VI, 150 |
| 5:9 | VI, 267 |

II PETER

| | |
|---|---|
| 1:10–11 | III, 300 f. |
| 1:16–18 | V, 86–94 |
| 1:20 | I, 118 |
| 1:20–21 | VI, 32 |
| 1:21 | I, 80 f.; VI, 53, 75 |
| 2:1 | II, 106 |
| 2:1–22 | III, 294 |
| 3:3–4 | V, 306 f. |
| 3:7–13 | II, 369 ff. |
| 3:8 | V, 306 f. |
| 3:10–13 | V, 306 f. |

I JOHN

| | |
|---|---|
| 1:1—2:2 | III, 101 f., 328–31 |
| 1:2 | I, 297 |
| 1:4 | II, 334 |
| 1:5 | III, 262 |
| 1:5–7 | V, 147 |
| 1:5—2:2 | VI, 238 ff. |
| 1:6 | II, 72, 334 |
| 1:7 | II, 325, 337; III, 262; V, 197; VII, 54 |
| 1:8 | III, 96; VI, 271 f., 288 |
| 1:9 | II, 336 f.; III, 388; VII, 84 f. |
| 1:10 | III, 96 f.; VI, 272 |
| 2:1 | II, 342 ff. |
| 2:1–2 | V, 277; VII, 163 f. |
| 2:2 | II, 327 f., 337; III, 95 f.; V, 197 f. |

| | |
|---|---|
| 2:15 | VI, 202 |
| 2:19 | III, 271 f. |
| 2:20 | VI, 134 |
| 2:27 | VI, 87 f., 125 f., 134 |
| 3:4–10 | II, 262–65, 268 |
| 3:9 | VI, 272 |
| 3:9–10 | VII, 22 |
| 3:10 | III, 301 |
| 3:16 | V, 198 |
| 3:20–22 | II, 199 |
| 3:24 | VI, 129 |
| 4:4 | I, 413 |
| 4:10 | V, 198 |
| 4:13 | VI, 129 |
| 5:4 | II, 330 |
| 5:4–5 | III, 306, 358; VI, 182 |
| 5:11–12 | V, 247 |
| 5:13 | VII, 24 |
| 5:16 | III, 310 |
| 5:19 | II, 82, 324; III, 215, 232 |

JUDE

| | |
|---|---|
| 1:3–19 | III, 294 f. |
| 1:9 | VI, 267 f. |
| 1:14–15 | II, 24; V, 289 |
| 1:24 | III, 364 |

REVELATION

| | |
|---|---|
| 1:5 | V, 199 |
| 1:8 | IV, 299 |
| 1:10 | VII, 109 |
| 1:19 | IV, 297 |
| 1:20 | II, 3 |
| 2:1—3:19 | IV, 352 f. |
| 3:10 | IV, 369 ff. |
| 3:14 | V, 26 |
| 4:4 | IV, 371 f. |
| 4:6—5:14 | II, 18 |
| 4:8 | I, 308 |
| 5:9 | V, 199 |
| 6:1—19:21 | IV, 342 f. |
| 7:1–8 | V, 123 |
| 7:14 | V, 199 f.; VII, 54 |
| 12:7–12 | II, 58 |
| 12:9 | II, 99 |
| 13:1–8 | IV, 350 f. |
| 13:1–10 | VII, 17 |
| 13:8 | I, 367; V, 200 f. |
| 17:1–18 | IV, 354–57 |
| 18:1–24 | IV, 357 ff. |
| 19:7–8 | IV, 131, 377 |
| 19:10 | IV, 298 |
| 19:11–16 | V, 307 ff. |
| 19:12 | VII, 210 |
| 19:15 | IV, 342 |
| 20:1–3 | II, 60 f. |
| 20:3 | V, 361 |
| 20:11—22:7 | II, 368 f. |
| 20:12 | III, 197 f. |
| 21:1—22:7 | IV, 131 |
| 21:4 | V, 363 |
| 21:8, 27 | III, 311 f. |
| 21:24–26 | IV, 6 |
| 22:16 | V, 329 |
| 22:18 | I, 93 |
| 22:19 | III, 305 f. |

# SUBJECT INDEX

# SUBJECT INDEX

## A

Abiding: VII, 3–6

Abraham: IV, 47–48, 288–89
  covenant: IV, 313–14; VII, 97
  headship: IV, 48
  physical seed in Israel: IV, 47–48
  prophet: IV, 288–89
  spiritual seed in faithful: IV, 47–48

Adam: VII, 6–9
  apostasy: VII, 19
  environment: II, 200–2
  N. T. doctrine: VII, 7–9, 113–14
  O. T. doctrine: VII, 6–7
  responsibility: II, 202
  temptation. historicity: II, 204–9
    nature: II, 209–14
  typical relation to Christ: VII, 7–9

Adamic nature: VI, 183, 269–75
  relation to Christ's death: VI, 276–278

Adoption: III, 242–43; VII, 9–11
  human: VII, 9
  spiritual: VII, 9–11

Advocacy: VII, 11–13

Ages. divine program: I, xi–xiii, 253–255
  divine program. Biblical evidence: I, xi–xiii
    relation to Systematic Theology: I, xi–xiii

Agnosticism: I, 130, 138–39, 164–66
  definition: I, 164–65

Amillennialism: IV, 281–82

Angel. definition: II, 3

Angel of Jehovah: I, 327–31; II, 20–21; V, 31–33; VII, 14
  deity: I, 327–31; V, 31–32
  one of Trinity: I, 329–31

Angelology: I, xxvi–xxix; II, 3–121; VII, 13–15
  heathen beliefs: II, 4–5
  history. Middle Ages: II, 4
  introduction: II, 3–5
  relation to reason: II, 3
  satanology and demonology: I, xxvii–xxix

Angels: IV, 5, 411, 415–16; VII, 13–15
  abode: II, 6–8, 14
  apostasy: VII, 18–19
  Biblical evidence: I, xxvii, 37, 308; II, 3
  cherubim. protectors of God's holiness: II, 17–18
  classification: II, 6–7, 16–21; VII, 14–15
    cherubim, seraphim, living creatures: II, 17–19
    elect angels: II, 17
    government rulers: II, 16–17
  creation: II, 11
  designated by ministry: II, 20
  existence. incorporeal: II, 12–13
    purpose: II, 11–12
  fall: II, 28–29
  Gabriel: II, 20
  general facts: II, 6–27
  governmental rulers. authorities: II, 16–17
    dominions: II, 16–17
    powers: II, 16–17
    principalities: II, 16–17
    thrones: II, 16–17
  influence to holiness: II, 30
  living creatures. identical with cherubim, seraphim: II, 19
  Lucifer, son of the morning: II, 19
  Michael: II, 19–20

Angels (*continued*)
  ministry: II, 21–24
    to Christ: II, 23–24
    to God: II, 21–22
    to men: II, 22–23
  number: II, 6, 15
  personality: II, 10–11
  power: II, 15–16
  progress in knowledge: II, 24–26
  reality: II, 8–9
  relation to men: II, 3–4, 9–10
  relation to moral problem: II, 28–32
  relation to redemption: II, 24–26
  scope of sin: II, 62
  self-determinative: II, 29–30
  seraphim. purifiers and worshipers: II, 18–19
  spectators of earthly scenes: II, 26–27
Animation: I, 120–23
  characteristics: I, 120–21
    power: I, 121
    vitality: I, 120–21
  definition: I, 120
  relation to believers: I, 122
  relation to unbelievers: I, 121–22
Annihilationism: IV, 420–22
Anthropology: II, 125–73; VII, 15–16
  introduction: II, 125–29
  Biblical. contrasts to secular: II, 125
    definition: II, 126
  secular: II, 126; VII, 15
Antichrist: VII, 16–17
Apostasy: III, 293–95; VII, 17–19, 111
  definition: VII, 17
Archaeology: I, 66
Armageddon: IV, 397
Arminianism: III, 182, 185, 268; VII, 137
Ascension: VII, 19–20
Assurance: VII, 21–24
  basis in Christian experience: VII, 21–23
  basis in Word of God: VII, 23–24

Astronomy: II, 6
  relation to reason: I, 134
Atheism: I, 163–64
  definition: I, 163–64
Atonement: III, 127, 135–64; VII, 25–27
  N. T. doctrine: VII, 26
  O. T. doctrine: VII, 25–26
  theological use: VII, 26–27
  theories. commercial: III, 67, 137–139
    identification: III, 142
    marturial: III, 141
    moral influence: III, 141–42
    payment to Satan: III, 136–37
    rectoral or governmental: III, 139, 142–54
    satisfaction: III, 154–64
    universalism: III, 140–41
Authority: VII, 27–29
  civil: VII, 29

B

Babylon: VII, 29–31
  commercial and political: VII, 31
  ecclesiastical: VII, 30–31
Baptism: VII, 32–43
  Christian. relation to baptism of Christ: V, 69–70
  meaning of word: VI, 138–40
  meanings of Greek words used: VII, 32–33
  Old Testament: V, 65–66; VII, 41
  relation to faith: III, 381–84
  ritual: VII, 34–43
    affusion: VII, 36
    immersion: VII, 36–37
    modes of: VII, 35
    prepositions used: VII, 39–40
    trine immersion: VII, 37
  Scriptures involved: VII, 39
  Spirit: III, 73–74, 99–100, 381–84
    meaning: II, 350
  spiritual: VI, 138–61; VII, 32–34, 36
    attributed to Christ: VI, 141–42

attributed to Holy Spirit: VI, 142–51
result. new creation: VI, 151–57
use of the word: VII, 38
Baptism of Infants: VII, 41–42
Baptism of John. Repentance: V, 63
Baptist. John the Baptist: VII, 41
Beatitudes: IV, 216–19; V, 103–5
Believers: I, 38–40, 308
Benedictions: I, 308–9
Bible
attitudes: I, 12–15
authority: I, 7, 22–23, 83–84, 89–104
sources: I, 94–104
Christ: I, 95–98
God-breathed: I, 94
power: I, 102–4
prophets: I, 98–101
public accreditation: I, 95
Holy Spirit: I, 94, 102
canon. formation: I, 89–93
canonicity: I, 89–104
covenants: I, 41–43
Abrahamic: I, 42
Adamic: I, 42
Davidic: I, 43, 360–61
Edenic: I, 42
Mosaic: I, 42–43
new (Church): I, 43
new (Israel): I, 43
Noahic: I, 42
Palestinian: I, 43
difficulties: I, 66–67
divisions: I, 36–47
dual authorship: I, 72–76
evidences. authority: VII, 29, 45–46
continuity: I, 29–30
ethics: I, 27–29, 35
hermeneutics: VII, 45, 203–5
inspiration: VI, 28–32; VII, 45, 200–1
principal Scriptures: VII, 200–1
knowledge of content. essential character: I, vi, 114
lifetime study: I, vi

literary character: I, 31–34
N. T. canon. closing: I, 93
formation: I, 91–92
N. T. prophets: III, 19–20
N. T. revelation. principles of interpretation: IV, 296–99
O. T. authority. congregation: I, 98
king: I, 98
Levites: I, 99
officials: I, 98–99
O. T. canon. closing: I, 92–93
formation: I, 90–91
O. T. judges: V, 333
O. T. prophets: III, 17–19
relation to secular knowledge: II, 126–29
revelation. creation: I, 26
God: I, 23–24
monotheism: I, 24
prophecy: I, 30–31
redemption: I, 26–27
sin: I, 26–28
Trinity: I, 24–26
the Father: I, 25
Holy Spirit: I, 25
the Son: I, 25
typology: I, 31
science and the Bible: I, 34–35
supernatural character: VI, 30–31
supernatural origin: I, 22–36
textual criticism: I, 87–88
time periods: I, 40–47
church: I, 46–47
Gentiles: I, 46
humanity: I, 40
kingdom of heaven: I, 44–45
prophetic: I, 43–44
use and value: II, 333
vivification: VII, 45
Bibliology: I, 21–125; VII, 43–46
introduction: I, 21–47
Blasphemy: VII, 46–48
N. T. doctrine: VII, 46–47
O. T. doctrine: VII, 46
Blindness: VII, 49–52
judicial: VII, 49–51
physical: VII, 49

Blindness (*continued*)
 spiritual: VII, 51–52
  carnal believers: VII, 52
  unbelievers: VII, 51–52
Blood: VII, 52–55
 cleansing: VII, 53–54
 sacrificial: VII, 52–53
Blood covenant: VII, 54
Body: VII, 55–57
 human: VII, 55–57
Bread: VII, 58–60
 general meaning of food: VII, 58
 typical meaning: VII, 58–59
 symbolic meaning: VII, 59–60
Bride: VII, 60–63
Bullingerism. Israel-bride error: IV, 127–28, 130–31
Buried: VII, 63–64

C

Calling, effectual: III, 168, 194, 210–211, 236, 349–50; VI, 251–53; VII, 65–68
 effectual. Arminian view: III, 276–278
Calvinism: III, 184–85, 267; VII, 137
Carnality: VII, 68–70, 107–8
 character: VII, 68–69
 relation to spiritual life: VII, 69–70
Catholic Church: I, 14
Cause. first: I, 146–47
Causation: I, 143–44
Chastisement: VII, 70–73
 divisions: VII, 71–73
  corrective: VII, 72
  enlarging: VII, 72
  preventative: VII, 71
  vindicative: VII, 72–73
Children. home government: IV, 200
Children of God: III, 252–53, 346–47
Christ
 ascension: I, 370; III, 16; IV, 118, 393; V, 252, 261–73; VII, 19–20, 81–82
  clouds of heaven: V, 268–73; VII, 20

entered heavenly sanctuary: V, 264–67
 first-fruits: V, 267–68
 prophecy: V, 269–71
 resurrection morn: V, 262–68; VII, 19–20
authority: VII, 28
baptism: V, 56–73; VII, 40–41, 79
 baptizer: V, 56–59
 cup: V, 72–73
 Holy Spirit: V, 71–72
 meaning: III, 26, 40–42
 mode: V, 63–69
  exegetical evidence: V, 66–69
  philological evidence: V, 64–66
 purpose. priestly consecration: V, 61–63
 relation to Christian baptism: V, 69–70
 theories: V, 59–63
  identification with Godly remnant: V, 61
  John's baptism unto repentance: V, 60–61
  separation as Messiah: V, 61
birth: V, 47–53
body: II, 158–59
burial: IV, 393; VII, 63–64, 81
childhood: V, 53–55; VII, 79
 subject to law: V, 53–54
commandments of: VII, 5–6, 226
confession of: VII, 88–89
Creator: I, 342–43
death: I, xvi–xvii, 306–7, 370; III, 8–9, 15–16, 43–54; IV, 32–33, 50, 392
 attitudes: III, 46–47
 cross. a stumbling block: III, 43
  foolishness: III, 43
  not the only saving instrument: III, 193–94
 crucifixion. crime: III, 45–48
  prophecy: V, 181–88
 for whom did He die?: III, 183–205
 God's sovereignty: III, 49–51, 52–53, 60–61

importance: III, 43–44, 55, 131–33

judgment: III, 220–22, 239–40, 249–50

participation of Trinity: III, 53–54

responsibility: III, 49–51
His own part: III, 50–51
part of the Father: III, 51–52
part of the Holy Spirit: III, 51
unified action of the three persons: III, 53–54

results: III, 55–115, 355–57
blessing on Gentiles: III, 108–109
believer's forgiveness and cleansing: III, 101–2
end of law: III, 76–86, 240–41, 342–45; IV, 164–65, 234–251
national salvation of Israel: III, 105–8
peace, III, 112–13
purification of things in heaven: III, 113–15
righteous judgments: III, 102–103
spoiling of principalities and powers: III, 109–11
substitution: III, 55–76, 199–201
meaning of Greek words: III, 56–57
taking away of precross sins: III, 103–5
testimony of Scripture: III, 201–5
universal gospel preaching: III, 194–95

types: III, 116–26
according to Scriptures: III, 125–26
miscellaneous: III, 124–25
O. T. general sacrifices: III, 119–20
O. T. prescribed sacrifices: III, 120–23

unique: III, 133–34
value. theories: III, 131–52
value to God: III, 51–52, 134–35

Deity: I, 318–20, 339–47, 383; V, 7–23; VII, 78
attributes: I, 340–42; V, 17–19
eternity: I, 340–41; V, 17–18
forgives sin: I, 343
immutability: I, 341; V, 18
omnipotence: I, 341; V, 18
omnipresence: I, 341–42; V, 19
omniscience: I, 341; V, 18–19
centrality: V, 8–9
consciousness: I, 391–92
denial: I, 278–80; V, 8–9
objections: I, 345–47
prerogatives: I, 342–45
relation to Christian life: I, 280
relation to God's love: I, 279
relation to redemption: I, 278–79
triune relationship: V, 22–23
works of God: V, 19–22
creation: V, 19–21, 23–27
forgiveness of sin: V, 21
judgment: V, 21–22
preservation: V, 21, 26
resurrection of dead: V, 21

divinity. sonship: III, 30–31
exaltation: IV, 135–36; V, 252, 274
genealogy: V, 48, 53; VII, 166–67
Head of Church: IV, 48, 68–78
headship: I, xxxvi, 358–59; VII, 182
humanity: I, 365–72, 383–84; II, 158–59; V, 47–48; VII, 57
early heresies: I, 265–66
essentials of human nature: I, 369
freedom from sin nature: V, 49, 77–78
limitations: I, 369–70
necessity: V, 49
prophecy: I, 367–68
New Testament: I, 368
Old Testament: I, 367–68
types: I, 367

Christ (*continued*)

hypostatic union: I, 72–75, 339–40, 365, 382–96; V, 48–49

definition: I, 382

deity: I, 383

deity and humanity preserved without confusion or alteration: I, 384–89

humanity: I, 383–84

relationships: I, 389–96

to believers: I, 395

to fallen angels: I, 392

to the Father: I, 389–90

to Himself: I, 390–92

to humanity: I, 392–93

to sin: I, 393

to sin nature: I, 393

to Spirit: I, 390

to unfallen angels: I, 392

structure of doctrine: I, 383–89

impeccability: I, 393–95; V, 50–51, 77–78

incarnation: VII, 57, 78–80, 194–96

interceding: I, 333

Judge: I, 343–44

kenosis: I, 373–81; VI, 257–58

condescension: I, 371–72, 374, 377–78

controversy: I, 373–74

humiliation: I, 371–72, 374, 378–79

interpretations: I, 379–81

"the form of God": I, 375–77

King: III, 17, 30, 33; V, 317–76; VII, 223

Kinsman-Redeemer: V, 83, 180

Last Adam: V, 49–51

relation to first Adam: V, 49–51, 77–78

life: I, 368–70

accusations of blasphemy: VII, 47

blasphemed by Jews: VII, 47

childhood: I, 391–92

human parentage: I, 368–69

ministry: I, 306

names: I, 368

obedience: III, 42–43

postresurrection ministry: I, 109–10

relation to Holy Spirit: V, 80

sufferings: III, 36–43

anticipation of death: III, 39–43

divine compassion: III, 38–39

outraged holiness: III, 37–38

washing disciples' feet: V, 146–48

love for believers: IV, 135–37

Messiahship: III, 39–43; IV, 300–302, 323, 392; V, 88–89, 315–358

millennial reign: I, 359–61

names: I, 332–38; V, 9–17, 28–33

Angel of Jehovah: V, 31–33

designations of eternal relationship: V, 9–12, 24

exact image: V, 11

First-Begotten or First-Born: V, 11–12, 24

image: V, 11, 24

Logos: V, 9–10

Only-Begotten: V, 10–11

Logos: III, 13–15, 21; VII, 227–228

Lord Jesus Christ: I, 337–38

Messiah: V, 28–31; VII, 236–37

Only-Begotten: VII, 245

primary designations of Deity: V, 12–17

God: I, 334–35; V, 12–13

Jehovah: I, 332–34; V, 13–17

Son of Abraham: III, 33

Son of David: III, 33

Son of God: I, 335–36; III, 30–31

Son of Man: I, 336–37; III, 31–32

nativity: V, 47–53

virgin birth: I, 354–55, 359

Person: I, 349–54, 382; III, 11–34

hypostatic union: III, 33–34

seven positions: III, 12–17

prayers: V, 160–61

pre-existence: I, 318–31, 350–51, 375; III, 12–15; V, 3–38; VII, 78
  Angel of Jehovah: I, 327–31
  Biblical implications: V, 33
  Biblical statements: V, 33–38
  major passages: I, 322–27, 374–375
present session in heaven: I, xxxv–xxxvii, 110–11, 370; V, 164–165, 273–79; VII, 82, 286
  advocacy: V, 198, 276–77; VII, 11–12, 164, 247
  Bestower of gifts: V, 275–76
  building: V, 277–78
  expecting: V, 278–79
  interceding: VI, 235–36
preserver: I, 343
Priest: III, 26–30
priesthood: I, xxxvi–xxxvii, 357–358; IV, 64–65, 300, 392; V, 82–83; VII, 20, 256
  Advocate: I, xxxvii
  entered heavenly sanctuary: V, 264–67
  intercessor: I, xxxvi
  prayer: VI, 152–54
  relation to session: V, 273–79
  spiritual gifts: I, xxxvi
  typology: V, 177–78, 267
Prophet: III, 17–26; V, 93–94, 95–169
  sufferings and death: V, 187–88
prophetic ministry: V, 95–169
raises dead: I, 343
receives worship: I, 344–45
relation to Church: IV, 45–46, 50, 54–143
  Bridegroom and Bride: IV, 127–143, 377, 396; VII, 61–63, 127, 182
  Cornerstone and stones of building: IV, 61–64
  Head and Body: IV, 68–78; V, 219–20, 252–53, 256–57, 274–75; VII, 33–34, 57, 127, 182

High Priest and kingdom of priests: IV, 64–68
Last Adam and New Creation: IV, 79–126; V, 143–44, 256–57
Shepherd and sheep: IV, 56–59
seven figures: VII, 60–61, 129–30
vine and branches: IV, 59–61, 99–100; V, 148–51; VII, 4–5
relation to Israel: IV, 50
resurrection: I, xvi–xvii, 307, 359–360, 370; III, 16, 327–28; IV, 32–33, 79–92, 93, 117, 124–26, 393; V, 231–60; VII, 266–68
  Christ's prophecies: V, 239–41
  commemorated by Lord's Day: V, 253–60
  Covenant Theology view: V, 231–34
  dispensational significance: V, 231–34
  First-Fruits: VII, 153–54
  importance: IV, 80
  necessary: IV, 83–84
  neglect: IV, 79–80
  neglect by Covenant Theology: V, 231–34, 253–54
  N. T. doctrine: V, 238–60
  O. T. implications: V, 234–38
  O. T. prophecies: V, 236–38
  present standard of power: V, 249–53
  produced new order of being: V, 244–45
  proof: IV, 81–83; V, 241–43
    Bible statement: IV, 83
    disciples' experience: IV, 81–82
    early church: IV, 82
    empty tomb: IV, 81
    eye-witnesses: IV, 82–83
    God's program: IV, 83
    His truthfulness: IV, 81
  prophecy of: IV, 84–85
  prophecy, N. T.: IV, 85
  prophecy, O. T.: IV, 84–85

Christ. resurrection (*continued*)
    purpose: IV, 91–92
    reality: IV, 90–91; V, 243–44,
        251–52
    reasons: IV, 85–90; V, 245–49
        become First-Fruits: IV, 89–
            90; V, 249
        become Head of Body: IV, 87–
            88
        become Head of Church: V,
            248
        bestow life: IV, 86–87
        empower: IV, 87
        fulfill Davidic Covenant: V,
            246–47
        fulfill prophecy: IV, 86
        His Person: IV, 85–86; V, 245
        result of justification: V, 248–
            249
        source of resurrection power:
            V, 247–48
    relation to death: V, 231
    relation to justification: IV, 88–
        89
    typology: V, 235–36
return for Church: V, 164–65, 355
rewarder: I, 343
second advent: I, 370
    destroy man of sin: II, 71–72
session: III, 16, 26, 328–34
Sonship: I, 25, 313–16; VII, 290
    theories: VII, 152
subjection to Father: I, 363–64
sufferings and death: III, 35–54; V,
        177–230; VII, 55, 80–81, 105–
        106, 115, 272, 298
    Christ's prophecy: V, 187–88
    Christian's share: VI, 275–82
    contrast between crucifixion and
        cross: III, 44–45
    Corinthian Epistles: V, 208–12
    demonstrate wisdom, power, and
        sacrifice of God: III, 52–53
    Epistle to the Hebrews: V, 225–
        229
    epistles of Paul: V, 201–24
    epistles of Peter: V, 224–25

First Epistle of John: V, 197–98
from men: III, 51
Galatians: V, 212–15
Gospel of John: V, 189–97
John the Baptist: V, 189–91
O. T. prophecy: V, 181–88
    doctrinal: V, 184–85
    historical: V, 181–84
pastoral epistles: V, 223–24
prison epistles: V, 215–23
relation to world: V, 189–91
relation to Israel: V, 194–95
revelation: V, 198–201
Romans: V, 201–8
synoptic history: V, 188–89
Thessalonian Epistles: V, 223
terminology: III, 127–30
theories of value: VII, 105–6
typology: V, 177–81
    Levitical offerings: V, 178–81
    tabernacle furniture: V, 178,
        180
value: VI, 292–93
    value to the Father: III, 51–52
vicarious sufferings in general:
    III, 57–61
teaching: I, xvi
    conversations: V, 169
    major discourses: III, 24–25; V,
        96–166
    parables: V, 166–69
temptation: II, 51–52, 94–95; V,
        74–84; VII, 302–3
    N. T. passages: V, 79
    relation to Christian: V, 81–84
    relation to God's purpose: V, 80–
        81
    relation to Holy Spirit: V, 79–81
    relation to Satan: V, 81
    sphere of humanity only: V, 76
Theanthropic Person: V, 51–53,
        182–83; VII, 196
transfiguration: V, 85–94; VII,
        305–6
    divine attestation: V, 93–94
    importance: V, 86–87
    purpose: V, 87–90

reality: V, 90
relation to Covenant Theology: V, 85
relation to Messianic kingdom: V, 85, 86–87, 88–90, 91–93
relation to premillennialism: V, 85
relation to second advent: V, 86–87
typical relation to Adam: VII, 7–9
virgin birth: VII, 196
Christ as advocate: III, 328–31
Christ as intercessor: III, 331–34; IV, 67; V, 276
Christ as mediator: III, 61–62; VII, 234–35
surrender: V, 368–76
Christ as prophet: IV, 31–32, 51, 289–290, 299–300
Christ as teacher: V, 95–169
Christian: VII, 73–75
abiding in Christ for fruit bearing: V, 148–51
bondslave: VI, 260–61
classifications: VI, 169–72
cleansing unto unbroken fellowship: V, 146–48
dedication of life: VI, 254–55
new relationship to God: V, 143–146
other names for: VII, 73–74
position in Christ: IV, 92–100; V, 144–46; VI, 152
position. sons of God: VI, 106–7, 110–11
relation to church leaders: IV, 199
relation to cosmos world system: IV, 195–97
relation to erring brother: IV, 200–1
relation to human government: IV, 196–97
relation to imputed sin: II, 358
relation to man's estate under sin: II, 358–59
relation to "old man": II, 348
relation to other believers: IV, 197–199

relation to Persons of Godhead: IV, 195
relation to Satan: IV, 195–96
relation to unsaved individuals: IV, 197
relation to weak brother: IV, 201–2
responsibility in spiritual life: VI, 162–298
introduction: VI, 162–76
self-judgment: IV, 403–4
sin nature: II, 345–58
judgment: IV, 403
two natures of: VI, 185–88
Christian life: III, 248–49, 355–63; IV, 28–29, 94–96, 186–202
Christlike character: IV, 193–94
divine enablement: IV, 188–94
superhuman character: IV, 186–88
opponents: II, 329–32; III, 357–61
devil: II, 331–32
flesh: II, 330–31
world: II, 330
provisions: II, 332–34
sin: II, 325–59
effects: II, 334–45
Christianity: VII, 75–77
Christians: IV, 12–14, 418
Christology: V, 3–376; VII, 78–83
introduction: IV, 3–7
Church
apostasy: VII, 19
authority as Christ's consort: IV, 135
beginning at Pentecost: IV, 45–46, 394
Body of Christ: I, xiii–xx
distinguished from Israel: I, xiv–xix
brides as types: VII, 62–63
character. a building: IV, 43, 61–64
a new creation: IV, 92–100
intercalary: IV, 40–42, 385–86
organism: IV, 36–143
Christ's prophecy of: IV, 43
distinguished from Israel: IV, 29–35, 47–53, 127–33
exaltation: IV, 135–36, 376–77, 395

Church (*continued*)
  glorification: IV, 136, 376–77, 395
  last days: IV, 374–75, 394
  names and titles: IV, 42
  nature: IV, 365–66
  N. T. use of word: IV, 37–40
  organism. history of doctrine: IV, 36–37
  present-day sectarianism: IV, 54, 147–49
  relation to Christ: IV, 54–143
    Bridegroom and Bride: IV, 127–143, 377, 396; VI, 81–82; VII, 61–63, 127, 182
    Cornerstone and stones of building: IV, 61–64
    Head and Body: IV, 68–78; VI, 81–82; VII, 33–34, 57, 127, 182
    High Priest and kingdom of priests: IV, 64–68
    Last Adam and New Creation: IV, 79–126; VI, 151–57
    seven figures: VII, 60–61, 129–130
    Shepherd and sheep: IV, 56–59
    Vine and branches: IV, 59–61, 99–100; VI, 164; VII, 4–5
  relation to great tribulation: IV, 364–73
  unity of believers: V, 157–60
Church government. forms of: VII, 131–32, 177
Cleansing: VII, 83–85
  of Christian: VII, 84–85, 108
  of unsaved: VII, 84
  O. T. doctrine: VII, 84
Commandments: VII, 85–88
  Christ: VII, 87–88
  Mosaic: VII, 86–87
Communion with Christ: VII, 3–6
Communion with God: VI, 163–65
Conduct of life. inherent law: I, xx
  systems: I, xxi–xxii
Confession: VII, 88–91
Confession of sin. New Testament: VII, 90–91

Old Testament: VII, 89–90
Conscience: VII, 91–93
Consecration. relation to faith: III, 384–88
Conversion: VII, 93–94
  distinguished from salvation: VII, 93–94
  Israel: IV, 320–22
Conviction: VII, 94–96
Cosmos: II, 76–90
  destruction: II, 89–90
  impotency: II, 88–89
  relation to Christian: II, 78–79, 87–88
  satanic character: II, 76–77, 84–86
  satanic control: II, 77, 79, 80–84, 114
  satanic development: II, 86–87
Cosmological argument. atheistic view: I, 144–45
Covenant of redemption: V, 27–28
Covenant people. relation to repentance: III, 375–76
Covenant Theology: IV, 156–57, 311; VII, 96–97, 122–23, 176
  view of Christ's resurrection: V, 231–34
Covenants: I, 42; IV, 49, 305–6; V, 27–28; VII, 96–99
  Abrahamic: IV, 313–14; V, 317–321; VII, 97
    eternal provisions: V, 318–21
    nation: V, 318–20
    possession of land: V, 320–21
  assured Messianic kingdom: V, 317–33
  Biblical: VII, 97–99
  Davidic: IV, 314; V, 321–33; VII, 98
    N. T. prophecies: V, 326–33
    O. T. prophecies: V, 321–26
    relation to resurrection of Christ: V, 246–47
  grace: I, 42; IV, 156, 229
  Mosaic: IV, 314; VII, 97–98
  new: VII, 98–99
  new with Israel: IV, 314–15, 325

Palestinian: IV, 317–23; VII, 98
redemption: I, 42
with Israel: IV, 313–28
works: I, 42; IV, 211–12, 228–29, 231–33, 246–47
annulled: IV, 246–47
Creation: I, 26, 253, 305–6; V, 19–21, 23–27; VII, 99–101, 108–9
new heavens and earth: V, 365–66
origin in God: I, 143
Creations. two. commemoration: IV, 100–24
Creeds: VII, 101–3
ecumenical: VII, 102
postreformation: VII, 102–3
Criticism. Biblical: VII, 103–4
Biblical. types: VII, 103–4
Cross: VII, 104–6
Christian: VII, 106
judgment: IV, 402–3; VII, 214

D

Daniel. prophet: IV, 289
Darkness: VII, 106–8
Day of Atonement: III, 122–23; VII, 64
Day of Christ: I, xvii; IV, 33; VII, 110–11
Day of God: IV, 401; VII, 112
Day of Jehovah: IV, 11–12, 33, 383–384, 398
Day of Lord: I, xvii; VII, 110
Days: VII, 108–12
Death: VII, 112–15
character as judgment: II, 153–55
judgment for sin: VII, 112–13
physical: VII, 113–14
second: VII, 114–15
spiritual: VII, 114
Decrees of God: I, 225–59
definition: I, 225, 232
divine appointment: I, 232
divine permission: I, 232, 236–38
eternity: I, 228–29
final: I, 237
first cause: I, 228

free: I, 229
immutable: I, 245
manifestations: I, 253–57
manifested in creation: I, 253
manifested in grace: I, 257
manifested in miracles: I, 256–57
manifested in prayer: I, 256
manifested in preservation: I, 255
manifested in program of ages: I, 253–55
manifested in providence: I, 255–56
objections: I, 237, 248–52
objection from God's justice: I, 249
objection from God's love: I, 249
objection from human suffering: I, 251–52
objection from fatalism: I, 251
objection that incentive curtailed: I, 250
objection that preaching becomes pointless: I, 250–51
objection that sin is compulsory: I, 249–50
order: III, 178–82
Arminian: III, 182, 278–79
infralapsarian: III, 180–81
sublapsarian: I, 246; III, 181
supralapsarian: I, 245; III, 179–180
perfection: I, 225–26
problem of will: I, 238
relation to election: I, 232
relation to moral agents: I, 230–31
relation to predestination: I, 232
relation to retribution: I, 232
relation to sin: I, 226–28, 232–38
relation to sovereignty: I, 226
unconditional: I, 229–30
wise: I, 229
Deism: I, 176
definition: I, 176
Demon possession: II, 119–21; VII, 117–18
relation to demon influence: II, 119, 121
Demonology: II, 113–21; VII, 115–118

Demonology (*continued*)
  heathen beliefs: II, 37
Demons. activity: II, 117
  character: II, 119–20; VII, 115–17
    bodiless spirits: II, 119; VII,
      115–16
    evil: II, 120
    seeking embodiment: II, 119–20;
      VII, 116
    wicked: VII, 116–17
  classes: II, 114
  identity: II, 113–14
  relation to Christ: II, 121
  relation to Satan: II, 113–14
  relation to spiritism: II, 117–18
  sin with daughters of men: II, 114–
    117
Depravity: II, 316–23; III, 166–67,
  211–17, 230–32, 359, 366; VI,
  290–91; VII, 107, 118–20, 156,
  241
  relation to Christian: II, 358–59
  remedy: II, 319–23
  spiritual blindness: I, 107, 129,
    162
Destruction of Jerusalem: V, 118–19
Disciples: VII, 120–21
  relation to apostles: VII, 120
  relation to believers: VII, 120–21
Dispensations. divine: IV, 16–21, 49,
  90, 100–2, 154–56, 205–8; V, 98–
  99, 254–57; VI, 100–2; VII,
  121–23
  Church: IV, 18–19, 113–22, 180–
    202, 205–7, 368–69, 386–87,
    393; V, 191, 255–56; VI, 80–
    84
    Gentile privilege: VI, 83–84
    intercalary character: VI, 81
    new divine purpose: VI, 81–82
    relation to evil: VI, 83
    relation to Israel: VI, 83
    witnessing: VI, 82
  conscience: I, 40
  definition: I, 40
  grace: I, 41
  Holy Spirit: VI, 123

human government: I, 40–41; VII,
  177
innocence: I, 40
kingdom: I, 41; IV, 19, 167–79,
  207–8; V, 256
law or Mosaic: I, 41; IV, 18, 102–
  113, 113–15, 158–66, 205; V,
  254–55
pre-Mosaic: IV, 157–58; V, 254
promise: I, 41
terms used: VII, 121–23
Divine nature. presence: III, 345–46
Divine purpose. execution: III, 347–
  351
Divine purposes: IV, 47, 73–74
Dualism: I, 177
  ethical: I, 177
  philosophical: I, 177
  psychological: I, 177
  theological: I, 177

E

Ecclesiology: IV, 3–251; VII, 127–30
  divisions: I, xiii; IV, 27–29
    Christian life: IV, 28–29, 154–
      251
    the church organically: IV, 27–
      28, 36–143
    the church organizationally: IV,
      28, 55–56, 144–53, 352–59
  introduction: IV, 3–35
Elders: VII, 130–32
  N. T. use of word: VII, 131
  types: VII, 132
Election: I, 232, 244–46; III, 165–
  205, 268–69, 347–48; VI, 91–93;
  VII, 132–38
  Abraham: III, 169–70
  Church: VII, 134–35
  Cyrus: III, 171
  essential truths: III, 172–76
  eternal character: III, 172–73, 234–
    236
  general doctrine: VII, 132–33
  immutable: III, 174–75
  Israel: VII, 133–34

objections: III, 176–77; VII, 135–136
  human will: VII, 136
  partiality: VII, 135–36
  relation to Christ's death: III, 175–176
  relation to foreknowledge: III, 173–174
  relation to mediation: III, 175
  relation to redemption: III, 187
  relation to retribution: I, 246–48
  revealed: III, 168–72
  terms used: III, 167–68
  universality: III, 165–66
  views: III, 184–85
  views of two Calvinist schools: III, 185–88
Elective decrees. order: VII, 137
Eradicationism: VI, 286–88
Eschatology: IV, 23–27, 255–439; VII, 111, 138–40
  introduction: IV, 255–63
Eternal life: IV, 24–26, 389, 400–1; VII, 142, 227
  Christian. possession: IV, 25–26
  Mosaic. inheritance: IV, 24–25
Eternal security: III, 267–370
  Arminian view: III, 273–312
    appeal to Scriptures: III, 290–312
    emphasis on human experience and reason: III, 286–90
    major soteriological doctrines: III, 275–85
  Arminius' view: III, 271
  Augustine's view: III, 270
  basis: III, 316–39
    baptism of Holy Spirit: III, 337–338
    Christ's advocacy: III, 328–31
    Christ's death: III, 326–27
    Christ's intercession: III, 331–34
    Christ's resurrection: III, 327–328
    God's love: III, 321–23
    God's omnipotence: III, 320–321
    God's response to Christ's prayer: III, 323–24
    God's sovereign purpose: III, 316–19
    indwelling by Holy Spirit: III, 336–37
    regeneration by Holy Spirit: III, 335–36
    sealing of Holy Spirit: III, 338–339
  Calvinistic view: III, 313–39
  consummating Scripture: III, 340–355
  introduction: III, 267–72
  Lutheran view: III, 271
Eternal state: IV, 389, 400–1, 413–39
  classes of persons: IV, 415–18
  spheres of existence: IV, 418–20
  theories: IV, 420–26
Eternity: VII, 140–42
  definition: VII, 141
  relation to time: VII, 141–42
Evangelism: VII, 142–46
  definition: VII, 143–45
  N. T. method: I, ix
  N. T. purpose: VII, 143–44
Evangelist. N. T. use of word: VII, 145–46
Evil. character in church age: VI, 83
  problem of origin: II, 28, 31–32
Evolution: I, 166–70; II, 130–35; VII, 99, 146, 149
  atheistic: I, 166, 169
  definition: I, 166
  man: I, 157
  naturalistic: II, 131
  theistic: I, 166; II, 131
  theory: I, 168
Expiation: III, 127

F

Faith: I, 11; VII, 146–48
  essential character: VI, 293–94
  gift of God: VII, 147
  meanings of word: VII, 148
  relation to baptism: III, 381–84

Faith (*continued*)
  relation to confessing Christ: III, 378–80
  relation to knowledge: VII, 147
  relation to repentance: III, 372–78
  relation to restitution: III, 388
  relation to special pleading: III, 389–92
  relation to surrender: III, 384–88
  relation to works: III, 297–302
Fall from grace: III, 310–11
Fall of man: I, 105; II, 215–23; VII, 16, 19, 149–50
  Arminian view: III, 279–80
  results: II, 215–16; VII, 16, 150
    depravity: II, 218–22
    physical death: II, 222–23
    spiritual death: II, 217–18
    subject to Satan: II, 217
Fellowship with God. loss of: III, 309–310
Filioque controversy: VI, 10–12
First-fruits: VII, 153–55
  Christ: VII, 153–54
  early Christians: VII, 154
  first believers in locality: VII, 154
  Holy Spirit: VII, 154
  Israel: VII, 154
  Kingdom believers: VII, 154–55
Flesh: VII, 155–57
  evil character: VII, 156
  N. T. uses of word: VI, 183, 269
  relation to Christian: VII, 155–57
  secret of victory: VI, 188–94
Foreknowledge: I, 230; VII, 158–60
  relation to decree: VII, 160
  relation to foreordination: VII, 158
  relation to omniscience: VII, 158
Foreordination: VII, 160–61
  relation to predestination: VII, 161
Forgiveness. human obligation: VII, 165
Forgiveness of sin: II, 270–73; III, 62–72, 128, 238–39, 328–31; IV, 21–22; V, 21; VI, 50–51; VII, 74, 89–91, 161–66
  basis: II, 271; IV, 21

Christian: III, 101–2, 238–39, 328–331; V, 146–48, 197–98; VI, 50–51, 236–50; VII, 84–85, 163–64
  human requirement: IV, 21–22
  Messianic kingdom: VII, 164–65
  New Testament: II, 272
  Old Testament: II, 271–72
  O. T. doctrine: VII, 162
  unsaved: VII, 84, 162–63
Freedom of the will: I, 238–44; VII, 136, 310
Free will in systems of theology: I, 231
Friends, society of: I, 13
Future life. theories concerning: IV, 420–26
Future punishment: IV, 427–33; VII, 260–62
Future state of wicked: VII, 108, 114–15

**G**

Genealogy: VII, 166–68
  Christ: VII, 166–67
General N. T. warnings: III, 305–6
Gentile times. limits: VII, 170–72
Gentiles: I, 37–38; IV, 5–6, 72–73, 329–44, 379–81, 388, 416; VI, 83–84; VII, 168–70
  national judgment: IV, 5–6, 341–344, 379–81
  N. T. warnings: III, 306
  origin: VII, 168
  times of: IV, 330–44, 379–81; VII, 170–72
Gifts, spiritual: IV, 68–69, 70–71; VI, 215–20
  definition: VI, 216
  purpose: VI, 217–20
Glorification: III, 364–70; IV, 122–126; VI, 283–84
Glory: VII, 172–73
God: VII, 173–75
  absolute character: I, 138–39
  anthropomorphisms: I, 181–82
  authority by creation: VII, 27–28

being and attributes: I, 147–49, 156, 158, 187–224
  agent and object required: I, 291–93
  constitutional: I, 212–24
  eternal activity: I, 291
  eternity: I, 216–17, 291; VII, 141
  freedom: I, 209
  glory: VII, 173–74
  goodness: I, 206–7
  grace: VII, 178
  holiness: I, 202–3; VII, 107, 188
  infinity: I, 215–16; VII, 199–200
  immutability: I, 217–19
  justice: I, 203–5; VII, 218
  love: I, 205–6; VII, 230–32
  mercy: VII, 235
  omnipotence: I, 209–12; VII, 243
  omnipresence: I, 219–22; VII, 243–44
  omniscience: I, 192–200; VII, 244–45
    Arminian view: III, 280–81
  personality: I, 191–212
  righteousness: VII, 270
  self-sufficiency: I, 293
  sensibility: I, 200–8
  simplicity: I, 213–14
  sovereignty: I, 222–23
    Arminian view: III, 281–82
  truth, I, 207–8
  uncreated: I, 146
  unity: I, 214–15
  will: I, 208–12; VII, 309
Biblical doctrine: I, 23–24
blasphemy against: VII, 47
Creator: I, 146–47
definition: I, 187; VII, 173–74
Fatherhood: I, 25, 311–17; IV, 50; VII, 151–53
  believers: I, 316–17; VII, 22, 152
  creation: I, 312–13; VII, 153
  intimate relationship: VII, 152
  Jews: I, 313

Lord Jesus Christ: I, 313–16; VII, 151–52
  headship: VII, 182
  knowledge of: I, 139, 179
names and titles: I, 260–71; VII, 174–75
  Adonai: I, 261, 262, 268–69; VII, 175
  Adonai Jehovah: I, 261, 269
  Almighty: I, 261
  compounds with El: I, 261; VII, 174
  compounds with Jehovah: I, 261
  Elohim: I, 261–62, 264–68
  El Elyon: I, 261, 269
  El Olam: I, 261, 269
  El Shaddai: I, 56, 261, 269
  full N. T. title. Father, Son, and Holy Spirit: I, 261, 270
  God of Hosts: I, 261
  Jehovah: I, 261–64; VII, 174–175, 207–8
  Jehovah Elohim: I, 261, 269
  Jehovah-jireh: I, 269
  Jehovah-nissi: I, 269
  Jehovah-raah: I, 269
  Jehovah-rapha: I, 269
  Jehovah Sabaoth: I, 261, 269
  Jehovah-shalom: I, 269
  Jehovah-shammah: I, 269
  Jehovah-tsidkenu: I, 269
  O. T. epithets: I, 269
  Second Person. Lord Jesus Christ: I, 261–62
  the First Person: I, 262
  the Second Person: I, 262
  the Third Person: I, 262
    the Spirit of Christ: I, 270
    the Spirit of God: I, 270
Person: I, 179–86
plurality. trinitarian: I, 294–95
saving work: III, 206–66
Spirit: I, 181–82
trinitarian name: VI, 7–19
  baptismal formula: VI, 9
Goodness. benevolence: I, 206
  complacency: I, 206

Goodness (*continued*)
grace: I, 206–7, 257
mercy: I, 206–7
Gospel: VII, 175–76
types: VII, 175–76
everlasting: VII, 176
grace of God: VII, 175–76
kingdom: VII, 175
Government: VII, 177–78
human: VII, 177
Grace: III, 225–66; VII, 178–79
age of: IV, 180–202
Arminian view: III, 282–85
basis. Christ's death: III, 225–28,
229–30
character in God: III, 59–60
common: VI, 88
definition: III, 50–51
distinguished from Kingdom teachings: IV, 213–25, 243–46
distinguished from law: IV, 180–81,
203–33
distinguished from love: VII, 178
distinguished from mercy: VII,
178
divine enablement to fulfill standards: IV, 188–94, 233
precepts of: IV, 184–85
relation to Christians: IV, 16
relation to Israel: IV, 15, 181–82
relationships: IV, 195–202
riches of: V, 191
character: III, 232–34
deliverance from power of darkness: III, 247–48
extent: III, 234–65
heavenly citizenship: III, 251–
252, 365
inheritance: III, 261–62
sons of God: III, 252–53, 346–47
second work of: VI, 122
superhuman standards of conduct:
IV, 186–88
teachings of: IV, 183, 185, 186–94
universal manifestation: IV, 182–
183
Guidance: VI, 225–28, 259–60

Guilt: II, 279–81; III, 128; VII, 179–
180

H

Hades: VII, 180–82
N. T. doctrine: VII, 181–82
O. T. doctrine: VII, 180–81
Headship: VII, 182–83
Healing: VII, 183–85
errors of divine healers: VII, 183–
185
relation to Christ's death: VII, 183–
184
Heart: VII, 185–86
Heaven: IV, 418–19, 433–39; VII,
186–87
abode of God: VII, 187
divisions: VII, 186
purification: III, 113–15
Hell: IV, 427–33
Heresy: VII, 17–18
Hermeneutics: I, 7, 8, 69, 114–19
definition: I, 115
principles: I, 115–19
context: I, 117
objectivity: I, 119
purpose of Bible: I, 115
purpose of each book: I, 116
recipients of message: I, 116–17
thorough exegesis: I, 118–19
total induction: I, 117–18
Holiness: VII, 188
Holy Spirit: I, 25, 397–414; VII, 291–
292
activity in millennium: VI, 60–62
attributes of God: VI, 23–26
eternity: VI, 23
faithfulness: VI, 24–25
holiness: VI, 25–26
love: VI, 24
omnipotence: VI, 23–24
omnipresence: VI, 24
omniscience: VI, 24
truthfulness: VI, 25
blasphemy against: I, 401–2; VII,
47–48, 165–66

character: I, 413
convicting work: I, 108, 412
deity: I, 399–402; VI, 3–4, 7, 22–46
  associated with God: I, 399–401
  attributes of God: I, 401
  called God: I, 399
  denied: I, 280–81
  relation to Christian life: I, 280–281
descriptive titles: VI, 19–21
fruit of: III, 361–62; VI, 199–215
  faithfulness: VI, 212–13
  gentleness: VI, 210–11
  goodness: VI, 211–12
  humility: VII, 190
  joy: VI, 207–8
  long-suffering: VI, 208–10
  love: VI, 202–6; VII, 230–32
  meekness: VI, 213–14
  peace: VI, 208
  self-control: VI, 214–15
gifts: VI, 215–20
governmental work: I, 404–7
grieved by sin: VI, 234–35
name: V, 7–21
neglect: VI, 4–6
N. T. evidence: I, 410–11
O. T. Abraham to Christ: VI, 70–79
O. T. Adam to Abraham: VI, 66–70
O. T. doctrine: VI, 66–79
O. T. evidence: I, 402–10
O. T. relation to individuals: I, 407–410
personality: I, 397–99; VI, 7, 9, 22
procession of: VI, 10–12
prophecies of: VI, 60–65
quenched by resisting: VI, 250–51
relation to Christian: I, 413; VI, 100–61
  introduction: VI, 100–3
relation to the Church: IV, 45–46, 50, 188–94, 372–73
relation to creation: I, 403–4
relation to devil: I, 412–13
relation to Father: I, 411
relation to flesh: I, 412

relation to Israel: IV, 50
relation to prophecy: VI, 57–65
  author: VI, 57–60
relation to Son: I, 411–12
relation to world: I, 412
relation to world system: VI, 85–99
relationships: I, 411–13
resistance to: VI, 253
titles: I, 411
types and symbols: VI, 47–56
  Abraham's servant: VI, 55–56
  dove: VI, 53–54
  fire: VI, 52
  oil: VI, 47–50
  water: VI, 50–51
  wind: VI, 52–53
work. advocate: VII, 12–13
  anointing or indwelling: VI, 40, 51, 74, 122–37, 158–59, 235
  baptizing: III, 72, 73, 337–38; V, 144; VI, 40–41, 51, 74, 138–161, 278–80; VII, 32–34, 36, 193–94
  baptizing Christ: V, 71–72
  convicting: III, 210–24; V, 152–154; VI, 33–34, 88–99; VII, 94–96, 145
  creating: VI, 27–28, 66–68
  earnest: VI, 46, 54
  empowering: III, 361–63
  filling: VI, 42, 74–75, 124, 159, 173–76
  fruit bearing: V, 148–51
  generating Christ: V, 49–50; VI, 32–33
  illuminating: I, 109–13; III, 212, 214, 217–23; V, 154–57; VI, 36–38, 221–25; VII, 45
  indwelling or anointing: I, 109, 111–12; II, 333–34; III, 263–64, 336–37, 345–46; IV, 188–94, 247; V, 148–149, 151–52; VI, 40, 51, 74, 122–37, 158–59, 235; VII, 22
  inspiring of Scriptures: VI, 28–32, 75–79

Holy Spirit. work (*continued*)
   intinterceding: V, 162–63; VI, 42–
     45, 229–30; VII, 202
   leading: VI, 225–28, 259–60
   O. T. sovereign enduement: VI,
     70–74, 130–31
   outpouring in millennium: VI,
     62–65
   paraclete: V, 151–52; VI, 38–39;
     VII, 247
   power for spiritual life: VI, 195–
     197
   praise and thanksgiving: VI,
     220–21
   regenerating: III, 241–42, 335–
     336; V, 144; VI, 35–36,
     104–21, 158
   restraining evil: I, 412; II, 71;
     IV, 372–73; VI, 34–35, 85–
     88
   revealing truth: VI, 69–70
   revealing future: VII, 138
   sanctifying: VI, 45–46
   sealing: III, 338–39; VI, 41–42,
     54–55, 74, 136–37
   security: VII, 286
   striving: VI, 28, 68
   teaching: I, 111–13; V, 154–57;
     VI, 221–25
   witnessing: VI, 39–40
   world-wide character: VI, 84
  works of God: VI, 26–46
Hope: VII, 189
Horn: VII, 189
Human conduct. systems of: V, 98–99
Humanity. divisions according to
  Paul: VI, 165–66
Humility: VII, 190

**I**

Idealism: I, 172–73
  definition: I, 172–73
Idols. blasphemy against: VII, 47
Illumination: I, vi, 9, 10, 105–13
  Holy Spirit: I, 109–13
  relation to inspiration: I, 50–51

relation to revelation: I, 50–51
Immortality: II, 152–53, 155; VII,
  190–91
  definition: VII, 190–91
Imputation: II, 296–315; VII, 191–
  194
  Adam's sin to human race: VII, 7–9,
    16, 113–14, 191–92
  Christ's righteousness to believer:
    III, 72, 74, 219–20, 243–44;
    V, 143–44, 201–3; VI, 96–97,
    154–56; VII, 75, 192–94, 220,
    270
  man's sin to Christ: III, 68–72;
    VII, 192
  theories: II, 310–12
Inability: III, 211–17, 385–86; VI,
  89–91, 104–6, 290–91; VII, 43–
  44, 51–52, 100, 144–45
Incarnation: I, 306, 348–64; III, 15;
  IV, 30–31, 392; V, 39–176; VII,
  57, 78–80, 194–96
  importance: V, 42
  introduction: V, 39–46
  Messianic purpose: IV, 30–31
  method: I, 354–55
  O. T. anticipation: V, 42–46, 54–55
    implications: V, 42–46
    prophecies: V, 44–45
    types: V, 43–44
  prophesied: IV, 304–5, 382–83
  purposes: I, xv, 355–64; VII, 195–
    196
    destroy works of Satan: I, 358
    faithful High Priest: I, 357–58
    Head of New Creation: I, 358–
      359
    Kinsman Redeemer: I, 361–64
    reveal God: I, 355–57
    reveal man: I, 357
    sit on David's throne: I, 359–61
  redemptive purpose: IV, 31
  relation to revelation: I, 58–59,
    355–57
  scope: V, 39
  the seed: IV, 302
Infant salvation: VII, 196–99

relation to election: VII, 199
Infinity: VII, 199–200
Inheritance: VII, 200
Innocence: VII, 200
Inspiration: I, 7, 22, 61–88, 307
    Biblical claims: I, 62–63, 67, 84–85
    character: I, 61–63
    definition: I, 61
    doctrine opposed: I, 61–62, 64–68
    dual authorship: I, 72–76
    importance: I, 63–64
    key passages: I, 76–85
    objections: I, 64–66
    relation to illumination: I, 50–51
    relation to revelation: I, 49–50
    theories: I, 68–72
        concept: I, 69
        degrees: I, 69
        dictation: I, 68
        mystical: I, 70–71
        natural: I, 70
        partial: I, 68–69
        verbal, plenary: I, 71–72
    verbal, plenary. objections: I, 85–88
Intercession: VII, 201–2
Intermediate state: II, 156; IV, 23,
    413–15; VII, 56–57, 202–3
    body of: IV, 414–15
    distinguished from soul sleep: IV,
        414
    locality: IV, 413–14
Interpretation: I, 114–19; VII, 45,
    203–5
    rules of: VII, 203–5
Intuition: I, 130–32
    character: I, 131
    definition: I, 130
    relation to theology: I, 130
    relation to tradition: I, 132–33
Israel: IV, 311–13, 381–82, 387, 390–
    391, 397, 399; VI, 83; VII, 205–
    206
    apostasy: VII, 19
    blessings: IV, 315–28
        eternal king: IV, 323
        eternal kingdom: IV, 324–25
        eternal land: IV, 317–23

eternal nation: IV, 315–17
eternal throne: IV, 323–24
calling: VII, 65
covenants: IV, 313–28
    Abrahamic: IV, 313–14
    Davidic: IV, 314
    Mosaic: IV, 314
    new: IV, 314–15, 325
    Palestinian: IV, 317–23
dispersions: VII, 123–27
    Assyrian and Babylonian: VII,
        124–25
    Egypt: VII, 124
    world-wide: VII, 125
distinguished from Church: IV, 29–
    35, 127–33
election: IV, 310, 316–17
judgment of: IV, 131–33, 317–18
national conversion: III, 105–8;
    IV, 320–22
relation to Jehovah. apostate wife:
    IV, 128–29
servants: IV, 52
repentance: IV, 318
restoration: III, 3–5; IV, 318–20;
    V, 290–91, 337–38; VII, 125–
    127

J

Jerusalem: VII, 208–10, 312
    destiny: VII, 209, 312
    new city of God: V, 366–68
Jesus: VII, 210
Jews: I, 38; IV, 6–12, 416–18
    covenants: IV, 7
    history: I, 46
    N. T. warnings: III, 302–5
    restoration: I, 106; V, 117–18, 136–
        140; VII, 50
    spiritual blindness: I, 105–7
John the Baptist: V, 56–59
    forerunner of Messiah: V, 57–59
    ministry: III, 27
        prophesied: V, 57
    Nazarite: V, 57
    priest: V, 59

John the Baptist (*continued*)
  prophet: IV, 290–94, 391–92; V,
    57–59
  supernatural birth: V, 57
Judaism: IV, 40, 158–66, 234–51,
    269–70; VII, 76, 137–38, 211–13
  annulled: IV, 248–49
  distinguished from Christianity: I,
    28–29; VII, 211–12
  divine disposition of: IV, 269–70
Judgment: IV, 402–12; V, 21–22,
    110–11; VI, 97–98; VII, 213–17
  angels: IV, 411; VII, 216
  Christian: IV, 377, 403–6; VI, 240–
    243
    chastisement: VII, 70–73, 214
    self-judgment: VII, 71, 214
    works: VII, 215
  cross: IV, 402–3
  Gentiles: V, 134–40; VI, 84; VII,
    168–69, 215–16
  great white throne: IV, 401, 411–
    412; V, 363–65; VII, 216–17
  Israel: IV, 131–33, 397, 399, 406–
    409; V, 110–11, 128–33; VI,
    83; VII, 215
    blindness: VII, 49–51
  Israel's oppressors: IV, 322–23,
    391, 399–400, 409–11
  Satan: VII, 96, 214
  sin nature: III, 96–101; VI, 188–
    191; VII, 36, 64, 156, 214,
    289
Judgment day: VII, 111
Just, the: VII, 217
Justice: VII, 218
Justification: III, 128–29, 245–46,
    325; V, 143; VII, 218–22
  Biblical doctrine: II, 273–78
  definition: VII, 219–20
  relation to forgiveness: II, 275, 278
  relation to imputed righteousness:
    II, 274–78
  relation to resurrection: IV, 88–
    89
  rests upon Christ's death: VII, 222
  work of God: VII, 218–19

K

King: VII, 223
Kingdom: VII, 223–25
  of Christ: IV, 26–27, 33–34, 378;
    V, 359–76; VII, 83
  of God: IV, 26–27; V, 315–17; VII,
    223
  of heaven: I, 44–45; V, 315–17;
    VII, 187, 223–25
  forms of: V, 333–58
  forms. consummate: V, 354–58
    Davidic kingdom: V, 333
    Judges: V, 333
    mystery: V, 349–54
    offered: V, 340–47
Knowledge of Scriptures: I, v–vii

L

Law: VII, 225–26
  deliverance: III, 342–45
  inherent: III, 78
Life: VII, 226–27
Logos: I, 58–59, 72–73; V, 9–10; VII,
    227–28
Lord's Day: IV, 113–22; V, 257–60;
    VII, 109–10, 228–29
  appointed under grace: IV, 115–16
  blessed of God: V, 258–59
  day of grace: V, 258
  distinguished from the Day of the
    Lord: IV, 116
  indicated by events: IV, 116–19
  individually committed: V, 259
  prophecy of: IV, 115–16; V, 257–
    258
  testimony of church fathers: IV,
    120–22
  testimony of church history: IV,
    122
  willingly observed: V, 259
Lord's Supper: VII, 229
Lost. estate: III, 230–32
Love: VII, 230–32
  divine. character. eternal: VI, 204
    character. sacrificial: VI, 204–5
    superhuman: VI, 206

unrequited and pure: VI, 205
objects. Church: VI, 204
    Israel: VI, 204
    world of men: VI, 203

## M

Man: I, 156–57; VII, 15–16
    constitution: II, 144–45
    creation: I, 3–6
        in image of God: I, 180–85; II,
            161; VII, 15
    headship: VII, 183
    immaterial nature: I, 156–57; II,
        160–99; VII, 15
        character: II, 161–73
        conscience: II, 197–99, 261–62
        constitution: II, 180–92
            dichotomous or trichotomous?:
                II, 180–92
            flesh: II, 188–91
            heart: II, 187–88
            mind: II, 191–92
            soul: II, 182–84
            spirit: II, 184–87
        creationism: II, 174–77
        intellect: II, 163, 193–94
        moral character: II, 163–66,
            202–3
        origin: II, 160–61
        original innocence: II, 162–63,
            200–14
        pre-existence: II, 173–74
        sensibility: II, 194
        Traducianism: II, 177–79
        will: II, 194–97
    indwelt by God: I, 307–8
    limitations: I, 129
    material nature: I, 156; VII, 15
        at creation: II, 144–59
        effect of fall: II, 148–49
        eschatology: II, 149–57
        meaning of the word body: II,
            157–58
        relation to sin: II, 157–58
        structure: II, 145–49
    origin: II, 130–43; VII, 15

creation: II, 135–38
evolutionary theory: II, 130–35
revelation: II, 135–38
time: II, 138–43
resurrection: I, 307
taught of God: I, 48
unsaved. relation to Satan: II, 64–
    65, 97–98, 99–101, 323–24
Man of sin: II, 40, 70–71, 95–97; IV,
    346–51, 397; V, 122, 296–97; VI,
    85–86; VII, 16–17, 232–33
Marriage: IV, 130, 199; VII, 233–34
Materialism: I, 144–45, 171–72
    definition: I, 171
Mediation: VII, 234–35
Mercy: VII, 235
    seat: VII, 236
Messiah: V, 28–31; VII, 236–37
    Deity: V, 28–31
Messianic kingdom: IV, 167–79, 207–
    208, 264–84, 290–94, 324–25,
    378, 383–84, 389, 400; V, 315–
    358; VII, 61–62, 82–83, 89, 91,
    111, 237–38
    announced: IV, 290–94
    assured by covenants: V, 317–33
    Christ's teaching: IV, 176–79, 214–
        224
    entrance requirements: V, 136–40
    inhabitants of: IV, 52, 219; V, 136–
        140, 337–39
    offered: IV, 265–66; V, 340–47
    postponement of: IV, 8–10, 174–76,
        266–67; V, 89–90, 91–93, 347–
        349
    illustrated: IV, 9–10
    prayer: IV, 221–22
    prophecy: IV, 168–79, 265
        New Testament: IV, 172–74,
            176–79
        Old Testament: IV, 168–72, 265
    prophesied character. centered at
        Jerusalem: V, 336–37
        earthly: V, 336
        established by returning king: V,
            339
        heavenly: V, 335–36

Messianic kingdom (*continued*)
  Israelitish: V, 337–38
  spiritual: V, 339–40
  theocratic: V, 334–35
  world-wide: V, 338–39
  prophecy of: V, 333–40
  realized: V, 354–58
  rejected: IV, 266–67; V, 347–49
Millennium: I, xvii
  Gentile participation: III, 108–9
Millennium and Millenarianism: VII,
  237–38
  amillennialism: VII, 237–38
  antimillennialism: IV, 281–82
  Church Fathers: IV, 270–77
  history: IV, 264–84
  N. T. teaching: IV, 257, 267–70
  original meaning: IV, 264–65
  postmillennialism: VII, 237
  postreformation consideration: IV,
    279–84
  premillennialism: IV, 282–84; VII,
    238
  Reformation. partial restoration:
    IV, 277–79
  Whitby's theory: IV, 280–81
Minister. authority: I, 307
Ministry: VII, 238–39
  training: I, ix–x; IV, 69
Miracles: I, 56, 256–57; V, 170–76;
  VII, 239
  New Testament: V, 171–72
  Old Testament: V, 171
Miracles of Christ: V, 170–76
  purpose: V, 172–73
  terms used: V, 174–76
Missions. Biblical teaching: IV, 50
Monism: I, 177
Monotheism: I, 24
Mosaic institutions. offerings: III,
  121–22
Mosaic Law: III, 77, 78; IV, 51, 158–
  166, 234–51; VII, 86–87, 225–26
  annulled: IV, 234–43
  application to Israel: IV, 165–66,
    236
  beginning at Sinai: IV, 162–64

Christ's interpretation: V, 105–8
  contrasts to kingdom teachings:
    IV, 213
  purpose: IV, 159, 161–62, 239–42;
    VI, 105, 273–74
  received by choice: IV, 162–64
  relation to time of reign: IV, 160–65
  similarity to kingdom teachings:
    IV, 211–13
  terminated with death of Christ: IV,
    164–65, 236
Moses. prophet: IV, 289
Mysteries. Biblical: IV, 75–77, 251,
  385–86
Mystery: VII, 239–40
Mysticism: I, 12–14
  Biblical: I, 14
  Christian: I, 13–14

**N**

Name: VII, 240
Natural man: VII, 241
Natural theology: I, 137–61
  anthropological argument: I, 155–
    158
  *argumentum a posteriori:* I, 141,
    142–58, 161
  *argumentum a priori:* I, 141–42,
    158–61
  cosmological argument: I, 142–49
  ontological argument: I, 158–60
  teleological argument: I, 149–55
Nirvana: IV, 426
Numbers: VII, 241–42

**O**

Obedience: VII, 242–43
"Old man" in the Christian: II, 348
Olivet Discourse: III, 24–25; V, 114–
  140
  relation to prophetic scope: V, 116
Omnipotence: VII, 243
Omnipresence: VII, 243–44
Omniscience: I, 192–200; VII, 244–
  245
  Archetypal: I, 193–94

Clarke's view: I, 195
definition: I, 192, 195
extent: I, 192–93
practical effect: I, 197–98
relation to foreknowledge: I, 192
relation to God's freedom: I, 197
relation to moral agents: I, 194–95, 196
relation to sin: I, 197
relation to wisdom: I, 198–200
Only-begotten: VII, 245
Ontology. definition: I, 158
Ordain: VII, 245–46
Ordinances: IV, 150–51; VII, 246
baptism: VII, 34–43
Lord's Supper: VII, 229
Organized church: IV, 144–53
government: IV, 150
forms of: IV, 150
group of local assemblies: IV, 152–153
local assembly: IV, 146–52
importance: IV, 144
N. T. teaching: IV, 145–46
order: IV, 151–52
ordinances: IV, 150–51
postmillennialism: IV, 144
Roman concept: IV, 144
service: IV, 149–50
without reference to locality: IV, 153

P

Pantheism: I, 173–76, 220–21
Buddhism: I, 173–74
definition: I, 173
Parables of Christ: V, 166–69, 351–54
kingdom parables: IV, 44
purpose: V, 166–68
types. general: V, 168–69
Messianic: V, 168
Paraclete: VII, 247
Paradise: VII, 247–48
Parousia: VII, 248
Partnership with Christ: III, 254–57
Passover, III, 120–21

Pauline Theology: VII, 248–49
revelation: IV, 3–4
doctrine of church: IV, 4
salvation by grace: IV, 3–4
Peace: III, 112–13; VII, 249
Pentecost: IV, 45–46, 393–94
Perfection: VI, 282–84; VII, 250
Bible use of word: VI, 283
positional: VI, 283
ultimate: VI, 283–84
Persecution: VII, 17–18
Philosophy and Christianity: I, 162–163
Pluralism: I, 178
Pneumatology: VI, 3–298
scope: VI, 3
Polygenism: II, 142
Polytheism: I, 172
definition: I, 172
Positivism: I, 176–77
Postmillennialism: IV, 280–81
Power: VII, 251
Praise: VII, 252
Prayer: I, 256; III, 257; VI, 107–8; VII, 22–23, 252–54
basis of: IV, 22–23
Christ's high priestly: VI, 152–54
intercessory: IV, 67; VII, 201–2
the kingdom prayer: V, 108–9
new ground in Christ: V, 160–64
relation to filling of Spirit: VI, 232–233
Prayers of Christ: V, 160–61
Preaching: VII, 254–55
Pre-adamitism: II, 142
Predestination: I, 232, 244–48; III, 168, 235–36, 347–51; VII, 255–256
relation to election: I, 232, 244–46
relation to retribution: I, 232, 244, 246–48
Premillennialism: IV, 282–84
Preservation: I, 55–56, 124–25, 255
Priesthood: VII, 256–57
N. T. doctrine: VII, 257
Old Testament: IV, 65–68
O. T. system: VII, 256

Priesthood of believers: III, 251; IV, 65–68

Profession of faith: III, 295–97

Prolegomena: I, 3–17

Prophecy: I, xxxii–xxxv, 30–31; V, 44–45; VII, 138–40, 257–58
    Biblical concept: IV, 285–95
    character. forth-telling: IV, 285–86
        predictive: IV, 285–86
    classification: IV, 294–95
    events in order: IV, 390–401
    extent: IV, 256
    fulfilled: I, xxxiv
    history: IV, 288–95
    major highways: IV, 296–378
        apostate Christendom: IV, 352–359
        Christ: IV, 296–309
        Church: IV, 374–78
        Gentiles: IV, 329–44
        Israel's covenants: IV, 310–28
        Satan, evil, man of sin: IV, 345–351
        great tribulation: IV, 360–73
    Messianic: IV, 7–9, 296–309
        two advents: IV, 302–9, 382–83
    neglect by theologians: IV, 255–56
    N. T. themes: IV, 385–89
    Olivet Discourse: V, 116
    O. T. themes: IV, 379–84
    primary emphasis: IV, 257
    relation to Christian life: IV, 261
    relation to covenants: IV, 288
    relation to eschatology: I, xxxiv
    relation to God's decree: IV, 261–63
    relation to hermeneutics: IV, 258–259
    relation to Holy Spirit: VI, 57–65
    tested by fulfillment: IV, 287–88
    unfulfilled: I, xxxiv–xxxv

Prophet: IV, 285–86
    election: IV, 287
    message: IV, 286–87
    New Testament: IV, 286
    Old Testament: IV, 286
    power: IV, 287

Prophets: I, 99–101

Abraham: IV, 288–89
Daniel: IV, 289
false: IV, 294
John the Baptist: IV, 290–94
Moses: IV, 289

Propitiation: III, 93–96, 190–93, 237–238, 389–92; V, 197–98; VII, 258–60
    N. T. doctrine: VII, 259–60
    O. T. doctrine: VII, 258–59

Protestantism: I, 15

Providence: I, 54–55, 255–56, 308
    definition: I, 54
    determinative: I, 255–56
    directive: I, 255
    permissive: I, 255
    preventative: I, 255

Providence and government of God: III, 348–51; VII, 177, 260

Punishment: II, 360–64; VII, 260–62
    relation to Christian: II, 360–61
        chastisement: II, 360–61
        scourging: II, 361
    retribution: II, 361–64

Purgatory: IV, 426

Purification. heaven: III, 113–15

Q

Quietism: I, 13, 14

R

Rationalism: III, 268
    Arminian emphasis: III, 286–90

Realism: I, 172–73
    definition: I, 173

Reason: I, 133–35
    achievements: I, 134–35
    value: I, 133–34

Reconciliation: III, 91–93, 129, 190–193, 237; V, 209–11, 221–23; VII, 26, 262–63

Redemption: I, 26, 27, 361–64; V, 212–15; VII, 263–64
    Biblical teaching: III, 66–67, 86–91, 129, 190–93, 236–37

extent: III, 183–205
  Arminian: III, 185
  dispensational aspects: III, 188–190
  extreme limited: III, 184
  F. W. Grant: III, 185
  moderate limited: III, 184
  moderate unlimited: III, 184–85
  N. T. doctrine: VII, 264
  O. T. doctrine: VII, 263–64
Redemption of body: VII, 56
Regeneration: III, 72, 73, 241–42, 335–36; VI, 104–21; VII, 74–75, 264–65
  acquisition of nature of God: VI, 109–10
  based on faith: VI, 113–21
  God's purpose: VI, 111–13
  impartation of life: VI, 106–9
  necessity of: VI, 104–6
  results. divine compassion for lost world: VI, 108–9
    knowledge of God: VI, 107
    new reality in prayer: VI, 107–8
    new reality in reading Bible: VI, 108
    recognition of God's family: VI, 108
Religion. contents: IV, 14
Repentance: VII, 265–66
  Israel: IV, 318
  meaning: III, 372–73
  relation to believing: III, 373–75
Restitutionism: IV, 423–26
Resurrection: IV, 23–24, 124–26; V, 21; VII, 8, 266–68
  Biblical doctrine: II, 149–57
  Christian: IV, 124–26, 375–76, 394–95
Retribution: I, 232, 244, 246–48
Revelation: I, 48–60, 135–36; VII, 44–45, 100–1, 268
  character: I, 51–52, 60
  definition: I, 48
  direct communication: I, 56–57
  extent: IV, 47
  modes: I, 53–60

progressive character: IV, 203–4
  relation to illumination: I, 50–51
  relation to inspiration: I, 49–50
  relation to reason: I, 48–49
  relation to theology: I, 135
Revelation and nature: I, 53–54
Reward. loss of: III, 307–9
Rewards: VII, 269
  Christian: IV, 396, 405
Righteousness: VII, 270
Romanism: I, 14–15
  error respecting the cross: III, 48

S

Sabbath: IV, 102–13; V, 254–57; VII, 109, 270–71
  annulled in church age: V, 255–56
  creation: IV, 102–3
  God's creative rest: V, 254
  institution as law: V, 254–55
  Jewish. character: IV, 105–6
    Christ's teaching: IV, 106–7
    prophecy of: IV, 111–12
    sign of Mosaic age: IV, 104–7
    teaching in Acts: IV, 108
    teaching in epistles: IV, 108–11
    unknown before Moses: IV, 103–104
  reinstituted in kingdom: V, 256
Sabellianism: VI, 14–16
Sacrifice. O. T.: III, 104–5, 129; VII, 271–72
Saint: VII, 272–73
Salvation: VII, 273–74
  basis: III, 8–9, 54, 208–9, 371–93
  gift of God: VI, 291–92
  God's motive: III, 7–8
  importance: III, 9–10
  meaning: III, 5–6
  means: III, 54
  Old Testament: III, 3–5, 105–8
    doctrine: VI, 73, 75
  results. deliverance from sin and human limitations: III, 355–63
    presented faultless: III, 364–70

Salvation (*continued*)
  scope: III, 6
  source: III, 6–7, 206–7
  terms: III, 371–93
    believe and be baptized: III, 381–84
    believe and confess Christ: III, 378–80
    believe and confess sin: III, 388
    believe and pray: III, 389–93
    believe and surrender to God: III, 384–88
    repent and believe: III, 372–78
  thirty-three miracles: III, 234–65
  trinitarian participation: III, 206–266
Sanctification: I, 308; VI, 45–46, 284–85; VII, 188, 220, 274–84
  Bible use of word: VI, 284
  experimental and progressive: VI, 284–85
  positional: III, 244–45; VI, 284
  ultimate: IV, 122–23; VI, 285
Satan: VII, 118, 284–85
  authority over the *cosmos:* II, 80–84
  Biblical evidence: II, 50–52
    New Testament: II, 51–52
    Old Testament: II, 50–51
  career: II, 39–61
  character: II, 62–75
    ambitious pride: II, 63–64
    antigod: II, 62
    antitruth: II, 62
    murderer: II, 65–66
    sinfulness: II, 72–75
    the lie: II, 68–69
    untruth: II, 64–72
  control of men: I, 107–8
  creation: II, 41–42
  fall: II, 35–36, 42–44
  final revolt: V, 360–61
  his doctrine: II, 106–11
  his sin: I, 239
  importance: II, 33–34
  judgment: III, 109–10, 359–60; IV, 345–46, 388–89, 399, 400, 403

  in cross: II, 53–57
  final: II, 43–44, 57–61, 208
    bound at second advent: II, 60–61
    cast into lake of fire: II, 61
    cast out of heaven: II, 58–60
  miracles: V, 170
  names and titles: II, 33
  opposition to Christian: III, 359–60
  original estate: II, 40–42
  original sin: II, 44–50
    character: II, 30–31, 43–44, 47–50, 93–94, 243–45
    motive: II, 94, 97
    personality: II, 34–35
    present abode: II, 45–46
  rebellion: VI, 255–56
  relation to Adam: II, 203–4
  relation to believer: II, 36, 101–3, 330; IV, 195–96; VI, 194–97, 266–68
  relation to religious cults: II, 110–111
  relation to unsaved: II, 323–24; VI, 90
  release at end of millennium: V, 360
  temptation of Christ: V, 80–81
Satanology: II, 33–12
  introduction: II, 33–38
  objections: II, 37–38
  satanic *cosmos:* II, 76–90
  Satan's method: II, 99–112
  Satan's motive: II, 91–98
Scriptures. Arminian interpretation: III, 290–312
  attitudes: I, 12
Second advent: I, 370; III, 16–17; IV, 51, 305–9, 318, 354, 377–78, 389, 398–99; V, 124–40, 280–314; VII, 82, 248
  certainty of fulfillment: V, 126–28
  distinction of comings: V, 288–314, 355
  events involved: IV, 306–7
  false theories: V, 282–87
  judgments of: V, 128–40, 290–314
  manner: V, 125–26

N. T. prophecies: V, 289–314
O. T. prophecies: V, 289–314
preview. transfiguration: V, 86–87,
    91–93, 303–5
return for Church: IV, 367–68,
    375–77; V, 164–65, 288–89
uncertainty of time: V, 128–33,
    305–6
Security: VII, 285–86
Sensibility: I, 200–8
    definition: I, 200
    demonstrated in nature: I, 201
    goodness: I, 206–7
    holiness: I, 202–3
    justice: I, 203–5
    love: I, 205–6
    modes: I, 202–8
    truth: I, 207–8
Separation: VII, 287
Sermon on the Mount: IV, 216–24; V,
    97–114
    beatitudes: V, 103–5
    criticism: V, 102
    distinctive character: V, 102–13
    postponement of application: V,
        113–14
    primary application in kingdom: V,
        99
    setting: V, 99–102
Servant of Jehovah: V, 184–85
Sin: I, 26, 233–38; III, 218–19; IV,
    346, 402–3; VI, 95–96, 184–85;
    VII, 287–89
    anticipated by God: II, 236–42
    Biblical doctrine: II, 224–73
    Biblical terms: II, 267–69
    Christian: I, xxiv–xxv, xxxvii
        effect upon God: II, 342–45
        effect upon self: II, 334–42
        prevention: II, 332–34; VI, 235–
            236
            Bible: VI, 235
            Christ interceding: VI, 235–36
            Holy Spirit indwelling: VI, 235
        remedy: II, 325–59; VI, 236–50
            chastisement: II, 360–61; VI,
                241–43

cleansing: VI, 236–40
confession and repentance: VI,
    243–50
    self-judgment: VI, 240–41
confession of: VII, 89–91
disposition: II, 365–73
divine remedy: II, 269–70
eradication: VI, 286–88
essential nature: I, 234–35
final triumph over all sin: II, 365–
    373
forgiveness of, for unregenerate: II,
    326–27
God's permission: I, 236–38; II,
    91–93, 229–33; III, 36
    reasons: II, 231–33
God's prevention: I, 234
imputed: II, 296–312
    divine remedy: II, 312–15
    relation to Christian: II, 358
    theories of imputation: II, 310–
        312
major demonstrations: II, 227–28
meaning of word: VI, 271–73
nature: II, 66–68, 224–27, 246–48,
    250–54
    always sinful: II, 326
    definitions: II, 254–55
    offense to God's Person: II, 255–
        260
    offense to God's laws: II, 260–67
    transgression of law: II, 260–67
    uncreated: I, 234
origin. anticipation in God's fore-
    knowledge: II, 236–42
    heaven: II, 242–43
    human: II, 248–50
original: II, 278–79, 283–95
    divine remedy: II, 292–95
    Arminian view: III, 279–80
    relation to Christian: II, 345–58
    relation to depravity: II, 285–92
    transmitted: II, 284–85
personal: II, 235–82
    definition: II, 254–67
    forgiveness: II, 270–73
    guilt: II, 279–81

Sin. personal (*continued*)
  origin: II, 235–51
    person who first sinned: II, 243–245
    relation to justification: II, 273–278
    terms. classifications: II, 267–69
  purpose in universe: I, 235–36
  redemption from: III, 86–90
  responsibility: I, 237
  relation to evil: II, 228–29, 242
  relation to free choice: II, 231
  relation to holy life: II, 328–29
  relation to "old man": II, 348
  relation to retribution: II, 361–64
  universality: II, 281–82
  unpardonable: VII, 47–48, 165–166
Sin unto death: VII, 166
Sins of saved and unsaved contrasted: II, 326
Socinianism: III, 273, 278–79
Son of Man: III, 31–32
Sonship: VII, 290
Soteriology: III, 3–396
  introduction: III, 3–10
Soul and spirit: VII, 290–91
Spiritual darkness. forms: I, 105
Spiritual gifts: V, 275–76
  evangelism: VII, 143
Spiritual life: V, 148–51; VI, 42, 123, 157, 162–298; VII, 3–6, 107–8, 130, 280–84, 292–93
  accomplished by Holy Spirit: VI, 177–78
  basis. sin nature judged: III, 96–101
  carnality: I, 108
  communion: IV, 60–61
  conditions to filling of Spirit: VI, 232–68
  conditions. negative: VI, 234–61
    grieve not Holy Spirit of God: VI, 234–50
    quench not Spirit: VI, 250–61
    walk in Spirit: VI, 261–68
    yieldedness: VI, 253–56
  dependence upon Holy Spirit: VI, 167–68, 261–68
  descriptive terms: VI, 173–76
  — example of Christ: VI, 256–59
  index. attitude to Bible: VI, 168–72
  life of faith: VI, 228–29
  methods: I, xxiii–xxiv
  motive: I, xxii
  necessity: I, 113
  opponents: VI, 178–97, 265–68
    flesh: VI, 183–94, 265–66; VII, 155–57
    Satan: VI, 194–97, 266–68
    world: VI, 179–82, 265
  related doctrines: VI, 269–89
  relation to Mosaic Law: VI, 166–67
  relation to surrender: VI, 172–73
  results. power to do good: VI, 198–231
    power to overcome evil: VI, 177–197
  standards: I, xxiii
  unceasing conflict: VI, 178–79
Spirituality: VII, 292–93
Standards of conduct. O. T.: IV, 154–166
Standing and state: VII, 293
Stewardship: VII, 293–95
Stone: VII, 295–96
Sublapsarianism: I, 246
Substitution: VII, 296–97
Suffering: VII, 71, 297–300
Supralapsarianism: I, 245–46
Symbolism. Biblical. blindness: VII, 49
  Biblical. bread: VII, 59–60

**T**

Tabernacle and temple: VII, 300–1
Teleology. etymology: I, 149
Temptation: VII, 301–3
  God: V, 75–76
  meaning: V, 74–75
    solicit to evil: V, 74–75
    test to prove virtue: V, 74–75
  sources of: III, 357–61

the devil: III, 359–60
the flesh: III, 359
the world: III, 358–59
Ten Commandments: IV, 208–11
Theism: I, 137–78
  definition: I, 136–37
  divisions: I, 139
    Biblical: I, 139–40, 179–271
    naturalistic: I, 139–42
  relation to Theology Proper: I, 137
Theologians: I, 6, 7, 8, 21
Theological education. curricula: I,
  viii
  curricula. English Bible: I, vii
    exegesis: I, vii
    purpose: I, vii
  task: I, ix–x
Theology. classifications: I, 4, 5
  etymology: I, 3
  science of. essential requirements:
    I, 7–12
  Systematic. abridged: I, x–xi
    definitions: I, x, 6
    divisions: I, 15–16
    modern decline: I, v
    relation to Bible: I, viii
    relation to missions: I, ix–x
    unabridged: I, 11–12
  uses of the word: I, 3–6
Theology Proper: I, 129–414
  antitheistic theories: I, 162–78
  definition: I, 129
  introduction: I, 129–36
Theophanies: V, 31–33
Throne: VII, 303
Tithing: VII, 304
Tongues: VII, 304–5
Tradition: I, 14, 15, 132–33
  relation to intuition: I, 132–33
  types: I, 132–33
    present: I, 132
    remote: I, 132
Transfiguration: VII, 305–6
  N. T. use: V, 85–86
Transmigration and reincarnation:
  IV, 420
Tribulation: VII, 306–7

Tribulation. great: IV, 10–11, 360–73,
  383, 388, 396–97; V, 114–15,
  120–25; VII, 108, 307
  nature: IV, 364–65
  relation to the church: IV, 364–73
Trinitarianism: I, 272–414
  definition: I, 136, 282
  denial of Christ's Deity: I, 278–80
  error of Sabellianism: I, 276
  error of tritheism: I, 275–76
  introduction: I, 272–88
  proofs: I, 289–310
    reason: I, 289–97
    revelation: I, 297–310
      New Testament: I, 302–10
      Old Testament: I, 298–302
  relation to Christ: I, 278
  relation to Holy Spirit: I, 280
  relation to Judaism: I, 287
  relation to Mohammedanism: I, 287
  relation to Scriptures: I, 281–82
  relation to Unitarians: I, 287
  term *person:* I, 276–77
  true emphasis: I, 286–88
Trinity: I, 24–26, 172, 272; V, 22–23;
  VI, 8; VII, 307
  analogies: I, 274–75
  assumed in Scripture: I, 297–98
  equality of members: VI, 12
  essential elements: I, 283
  general definition: I, 282–86
  mystery: I, 273–74, 288, 290
  N. T. doctrine: VI, 18
  N. T. evidence. attributes of God: I,
    304–5
    names of God: I, 303–4
    works of God: I, 305–8
    worship of God: I, 308–10
  objected as unreasonable: I, 274
  O. T. evidence. Deity ascribed to
    several: I, 299–300
    Elohim: I, 298–99
  O. T. implications: VI, 16–18
Tritheism: VI, 16
Typology: I, xxix–xxxii, 31; III, 116–
  26; IV, 46, 64–65, 119–20, 136–
  141; V, 43–44, 77–81; VI, 47–

Typology (*continued*)
    56; VII, 7–9, 19–20, 53–54, 58–
    59, 62–63, 64, 84, 193, 236, 296–
    297, 300, 308–9
    Christ: I, xxx
    Kinsman Redeemer: I, 361–64
    Church. Eve: IV, 137–39
    Rebekah: IV, 139–41
    death of Christ: V, 77–81
    definition: I, xxx
    meaning: III, 116–18
    O. T. sacrifices: III, 119–23
    principles: I, xxx–xxxi
    scope: III, 118–19

**U**

Unbelievers. children of disobedience:
    II, 65
Understanding. human. limitations: I,
    233–34
Union with Christ: III, 72–76, 228–
    229, 239–40, 243–45; IV, 60–61,
    92–100; VI, 152, 156–57, 163–
    165, 278–80; VII, 3, 33–34
Unitarianism: VI, 14
Universalism: IV, 422–23
Universe. destruction of: V, 362–63

    preservation of: V, 21, 26
    theories of its cause: I, 142
Upper Room Discourse: I, 110–11;
    III, 25; V, 140–66

**V**

Virgin birth: V, 47–53

**W**

Walk. relation to spiritual life: I, xx–
    xxvi
Will: I, 208–12; VII, 309–10
    characteristics: I, 209–12
    definition: I, 208
    free: I, 209
    man's consciousness of it: I, 241–43
    omnipotence: I, 209–12
Witness-bearing: IV, 70; VI, 82
Woman: VII, 310–11
World: III, 358–59; VII, 311–12
    N. T. uses of word: VI, 180
    Satan-controlled: VI, 179
    secret of victory: VI, 181–82

**Z**

Zion: VII, 312